ROOM 939

15 MINUTES OF HORROR, 20 YEARS OF HEALING

JENNY LYNN ANDERSON
with Ric Mandes

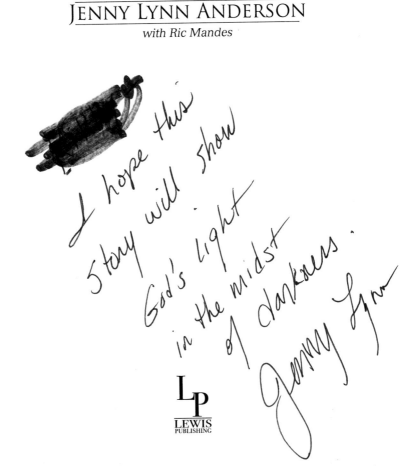

I hope this story will show God's light in the midst of darkness.

Jenny Lynn

LP
LEWIS
PUBLISHING

CONTACT JENNY LYNN

To book Jenny Lynn Anderson for an event
or for more information visit

www.jennylynnanderson.com

Unless otherwise noted, Scripture quotations are from the HOLY BIBLE: NEW
INTERNATIONAL VERSION. Copyright 1973, 1978, 1984 by International Bible
Society. Used by permission of Zondervan Publishers, Inc., Wheaton, Illinois
60189. All rights reserved.
Galatians 2:20 is from the King James Version (public domain).

Published in Statesboro, Georgia, Lewis Printing Company.
The Publisher is not responsible for websites (or their content) that are not owned
by the Publisher.

Library of Congress Cataloguing-in-Publication Data

Jenny Lynn Anderson

Creative Design by Rebecca Williams.

Photography by Stephanie Halley and Frank Fortune.

QR Codes by James Kicklighter, Greg Carter, Judson Crane,
Archie Jordan, Robin Holmes Lanier, Carol Thompson,
Morgan Anderson, Laura Milner.

ISBN-10: 0983992304

ISBN-13: 9780983992301

PRINTED IN THE UNITED STATES OF AMERICA

QR Codes

This book contains 6 QR Codes; each features content to enhance your reading experience. Each Code is a little audio, or video, gift from me to you.

To access this content, you will need to scan the Code using a QR Code Reader app on your mobile device. If you do not have a QR Code Reader on your device, please download one now from your device's app marketplace.

If you do not have a device equipped to read QR Codes, you can experience this content on my website: http://www. jennylynnanderson.com/qrcodes

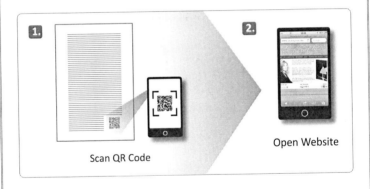

Scan QR Code

Open Website

Test your QR Code Reader here
to access my website,
www.jennylynnanderson.com

Dedicated to...

... my mother Faye Sanders Martin who instilled perseverance and courage in me, to my sister Janna Martin Friedman for her insightfulness and love, to my husband and best friend Mark Anderson who was my constant protector and fortress, and to my daughters Morgan and Allison who are the wind beneath my wings.

Foreword

I remember holding my second daughter just minutes after her arrival on that warm June afternoon of 1963. As her father Hollis and our 16-month-old daughter, Janna, took in the sweetness of our newborn, I heard the stentorian voice of my doctor, Albert Deal, asking, "What should I put on the birth certificate?" My Monday's child, blue-eyed and fair of face, was as yet unnamed.

That evening I prayed to God for the perfect name, one as joyful and beautiful as my new little girl; and in the night it came: Jenny Lynn.

Jenny Lynn's childhood was like that of a butterfly, gathering nectar and spreading happiness to all who knew her. "Mama, mama, mama" she would chatter excitedly, capturing a moment of my attention in the evenings after my workday ended as an attorney and, later, a circuit trial judge. Oh, how my imaginative daughter embraced life! "Mama, mama, mama," she would exclaim as she entertained me with narratives of that day's new adventure.

But adventures always have the potential for danger. I realized this as I held my daughter on a cold November morning 27 years later. Only this time she was sobbing. "Mama, mama, mama" she cried, her once-luminous face now stained with tears and creased with fear. Our Jenny Lynn had been assaulted in an Atlanta hotel while attending her first conference as public relations director for Willingway Hospital, a center for the treatment of addictions located in Statesboro, Georgia.

I wish with all my heart I did not have to write these words about the 15 minutes in Room 939. It stripped my daughter of her dignity, independence, and trust, thus imprisoning her in paralyzed fear for 20 years.

I applaud her will and determination to work through the darkness, to forgive, encouraging victims of such devastating crimes to come forth and release their pain.

So read of her life, torn to hell and back. The assault's effect on her marriage and family. How fear robbed her of freedom and stripped away God's rightful design for her life.

Thankfully forgiveness liberated my Jenny Lynn. My butterfly is back.

– Faye Sanders Martin

Contents

Contents

Acknowledgments

A grateful and heartfelt thank you to spiritual leaders and teachers Dr. John Waters, Dr. Bill Perry, Elder Randy Waters, the late Elder George Daunhauer, Elder John Shelton Mikell, Elder Bill Durrence, Elder Pat McCoy, Emily Fennell, Johnnie Ellis, Martha Green, Janet McGinn, Beth Stubbs, Jean Berry, Hazel Minick, Ida Waters, Gerri Deal, Wayne Brannen, Lindsay Walker, Kathy Rushing, Greg Proctor, Tyson Davis, Anne-Marie Aldred, and Andy Aldred for teaching me to love and trust God.

My sincerest appreciation to media professionals Jim Healy, Jenny Foss, Jenifer Andrews, Dal Cannady, Josh Aubrey, Martha Nesbitt, Elena Fodera, Linda Sickler, and Holli Deal Bragg ... who lifted my story and delivered it for all to see.

My deepest love and respect for the Mooney family, the late Dr. John and Dot Mooney, Dr. Al and Jane Mooney, Jimmy and Robbin Mooney, Dr. Bobby and Cindy Mooney, Carol Lind Mooney Bryan and Dr. Robert Bryan for being ever constant. And to the larger Willingway Hospital family, I will always remember you for loving me back to health and teaching me the Serenity Prayer: "God, grant me the serenity to accept the things I cannot change, Courage to change the things I can, And wisdom to know the difference."

And to Rodney Battles, my gratefulness for being by my side.

I simply could not have made it without the compassion of Dr. Al Palmer, Dr. Carla Branch, Dr. Randy Smith, Dr. Ellen Emerson, Dr. Michael Lichtman, and Dr. Jack Rainer ... Ashby Garner, Edie Mercado, Fred Richter,

Stephanie Tames, and Jason Wolfe who ministered to the healing of my body, mind and soul physically and holistically.

Glory be to God's disciples Deidre Nelson, Alice Mathews, Devra Walker, and Janet Mallard – who from the beginning supported me unconditionally through His love. Further, my walk was strengthened by spiritual warriors Liz O'Neal and Sarah Walker. Finally, Frank Hook whose words and heartfelt prayer in his Georgia Southern University office added to my strength and conviction at a time I doubted my ability to reveal all dimensions of my pain and suffering.

In life, we are blessed with endearing, everlasting friends who see us through the good and the bad, the tough and the tender. With that I would like to acknowledge that circle: Jill Nevil, Diane DeLoach, Kelli Mock Heartsill, Tracy Joiner, Dawn and Andy Oliver, Devra and Lindsay Walker, Alice and Harry Mathews, Cindy and Bill Sheppard, Janna and Tom Blackwell, Susan and David Brown, Janet and Richard Mallard, Kristen and Wayne Akins, Lisa and John Lee, Dawn and Michael Mallard, Deidre and Ed Nelson. Special thanks to childhood friends Beth Brannen Chandler, Sandra Thackston Paris, Becky Newton Miller, Jessica Johnston Klepchick, Angie Anderson Lee, Pam Newton Drew and Julie Winskie Schwartz for being that never ending beacon, lighting my way through troubled waters. And to all my Statesboro friends who have supported me throughout this project.

To the creative genius of Tynicka Battle, Judson Crane, James Kicklighter, Greg Carter, Robin Holmes Lanier, Archie Jordan, Carol Thompson and to my image makers Scott Durden, Amanda Clayton, Tommy Powell, Alisha Davis, Ashton McCullough, Paula Williams, Betty Newton.

I stand blessed and amazed at your insight. Each of you has brought a new and amazing dimension to my story. And for that you are hallmark figures.

A special thanks to Morgan Anderson, Allison Anderson and Lisa Toole for helping me frame the QR code which visually captured my emotions for this important chapter in the book.

A special thanks to Tommy Lewis and Jason Rogers of Lewis Color for believing in and partnering with this project to create and produce a multi-dimensional book that will help readers in their journey to healing.

Oh my, Sarah Russell, your willingness to tackle any task for me, no matter what size, blessed this entire journey. I cherished your replies as you headed out, "anything else?"

Rebecca Williams, my talented graphic designer, all I can say to you is though you are the resident of our South Georgia community, your originality and bold strokes have received accolades from here to Atlanta and on to New York City as your book jacket design enforces so strongly my story and reflects the drama of my nightmare and the angelic form of my healing.

A heartfelt thank you to Carolyn Mandes for her finale of proofreading the manuscript. Our Associate Editor Pat Murphey. You were heaven sent. Although we were strangers that first day we met at Longhorn's, there is no doubt it was through God you always took literary residence of those voids which will haunt a writer. You were a dweller of my soul. Through you this book came to life as you blessed each page with His Holy Spirit.

Ric Mandes ... It started over a bowl of oatmeal at Starbucks. Little did we know of God's plan for us. It came to life when you said simply "Jenny Lynn, you have a story to tell." And I did. And I have now shared it with the world. Thank you for being His messenger ... the Editor I needed by my side on both the calm and stormy days. And most importantly, reminding me daily God is our Publisher.

To my Anderson family, Mrs. Merle, Gary and Betsy, Lisa and Moses, Lori and Robbie, thank you for your love since 1986.

To Jone Martin Bremer, you have always been my inspiration.

To my mother Faye Sanders Martin, sister Janna Martin and brother-in-law Stan Friedman. You believed in my dreams and my journey of healing and were there for me for 20 years to find my voice midst the oppression.

This book could not have been written without the support and love of my faithful husband Mark, and daughters Morgan and Allison, who allowed me the solitude for that long season as I searched for the spiritual handrail leading to restoration. As you waited patiently, I know you often wondered if the wife and mother you knew and needed would ever return. You are the crew who never gave up on me. Though captured in fear, I always felt your presence, heard your caring voices. With God's love you were my choir who kept the anthem going until I returned ... free and whole again. Now I join you in our song of love as a family.

Morning Sky

In total darkness I wait for him
Searching the horizon dark and grim
Only emptiness, not there.
Black is the morning sky.

A solid canvas with no form
Endless world that is the storm
That keeps my eyes On him.
Black is the morning sky.

I search for hope in bits and specks
Always waiting for the flecks
A hint of promise for my life.
Black is the morning sky.

With no plan I do run
Back to that in which I turn
To the night where darkness churned.
Black is the morning sky.

Only emptiness of a tomb
Shadows of the doom
That keep me bound in his chains.
Black is the morning sky.

But Gray fills the void of night
A glimpse of soft and radiant light
A promise of my future and end of him.
Light is the Morning Sky.

J.L.

Prologue

Tybee Island, Georgia

Before I could write this book, I had to come to terms with one major obstacle. I knew the man who attacked me could possibly still be out there – find me, and finish the crime he started the evening of November 28, 1990. For 20 years, I remained captured in a state of terror. However, in the fall of 2010, friend and mentor Ric Mandes looked at me over a cup of Starbucks coffee and said, "Jenny Lynn, it is time."

Was it time, I asked myself? Did I have the courage to revisit 939 and the strength to bring life to that terrible journey once again? Could I face the demons I would unearth?

For several weeks I prayed, knowing I would need the spiritual power found in His Word.

God's answer came the morning of November 13, 2010, on Tybee Island, Georgia at 6:15 a.m.

I am sitting on the back porch of our beach house. The roar of the ocean fills me. Its waves begin washing away fear. I am left with a spiritual awareness of stillness and tranquility. The birds' chorus completes His arrival. The sun begins its ascent, leaving a trail of orange where earth meets sky.

There are tears. I taste their saltiness. A gentle breeze suddenly becomes a wisp of wind lifting a page of my Bible to this verse. "God is light; in Him there is no darkness at all" (John 1: 5).

I close my eyes. I am embraced by His presence. The fear is gone. I can breathe again. I can finally tell my story.

1

Going Places

In November, 1990, the Southeastern Conference on Alcohol and Drugs (SECAD) chose Atlanta as the site for its annual national conference and tradeshow exhibition. This was the premier forum that attracted counselors and professionals representing alcohol and drug treatment programs from throughout the United States. I attended the meeting as a marketing representative for Willingway Hospital, a nationally noted drug and alcohol rehab center located in Statesboro, Georgia. As the hospital's Public Relations Director and an aspiring journalist, I looked forward to an exciting and challenging opportunity.

Held at one of Atlanta's major downtown hotels, the activities began at noon on a Wednesday and were scheduled to end Saturday. On Thursday evening, after a day of enlightened seminars and workshops, Willingway's Marketing Director Rodney Battles and I left the hotel's exhibit hall, returning to our rooms to catch our breath and freshen up. We agreed our time out to be no more than fifteen minutes as we had invited selected trade magazine colleagues for dinner. While Rodney was interested in advertising placement and rates, I was excited about the prospect of pitching story ideas to publication editors. I intended to make an impact during those first 90 days as a member of the Willingway team.

We took the elevator to our floors with Rodney stepping onto the 4th as I continued onto the 9th. I was pleased to be booked in 939, a corner room allowing me expansive views of the south and east profiles of Atlanta. Eagerly anticipating the possibilities that lay ahead for the evening, I remembered how much I enjoyed traveling and the excitement of a metropolitan setting.

Thursday, November 28, 1990, had been a day of promise and opportunity. Accentuated by low humidity, crisp air and clear blue skies, it was a "great hair day," a blessing for Southern belles. These thoughts filled my mind as I moved toward 939.

It would be the last time I would feel safe walking alone.

2

Room 939

Adorned with fresh lipstick and a handbag over my shoulder, I closed the door behind me at 8:00 p.m. and headed for the lobby. Putting the hotel keycard in my pocketbook, I was satisfied I had everything secure in my bag. Then, I looked up and saw a black man moving toward me. I guess my woman's intuition was in the "off mode" because no alarms sounded – no quickened pulse, no surge of adrenaline. Some say a chill accompanies the entrance of evil into one's presence. If so, I didn't notice it. I had no reason to believe he wasn't just an ordinary guy walking down the hall, dressed in a dark leather jacket, jeans and a newsboy cap. But then we locked eyes – and he pounced.

My immediate reaction was defiance. Mom's solid rules about protecting myself came alive: "Be tough. Take them on. Do anything in your power to maintain your safety."

I couldn't believe this dark shadow was intent on doing harm. I actually thought, *"You have **got** to be kidding!"*

Then, just as suddenly as he had attacked, this demure lady transformed into a "kick butt" woman headed straight at him. He was medium build, around 5' 9" and 160 pounds at the most. I believed or hoped I could hold my own and at least get past him. Having excelled as a teenage athlete – co-captain of the cheerleading squad, a tenacious basketball hawk never afraid to "take it to the hoop," and an "in-your-face" tennis competitor – the fire in my belly roared to life.

"*Idiot*," I thought. "*You're messing with the **wrong** lady. You want war, you've got it.*"

But that flame quickly became a flicker as the gleam of a switchblade became the only relevant factor in a suddenly dark and lonely universe, as he snarled the first of his many commandments I would come to fear:

"Go back to your room."

This is it Jenny Lynn, You've got about a second to save yourself.

As I lunged and began grappling with him, my screams ricocheted from ceilings to walls and roared down the hallway pleading for help, only to be seemingly sucked up by some black hole, perhaps the pit that had spawned this fiend. Viciously he slammed me against the wall. Held now with brute force, I saw my chances for escape dissolve like my futile cries had only a moment before. I was powerless as he inched me with determination toward my room.

Still, not all the fight had left me. I dug my spiked, high heels into the carpeted hall, still hoping for an opening, a chance of release. Even with my body now tightly entrapped, my spirit roared like a cornered lioness. But the chill of that cold blade against my throat smothered the last dying ember of resistance. My muffled pleas became futile, as he growled, "If you don't shut up, I'm going to kill you."

In front of 939, with my body welded to the door, I could feel the raging steam from his hot breath on the back of my neck. As he slowly drew the knife even tighter to my throat, his next cold-blooded command confirmed my capture: "Put the card in the door."

I had lost the battle.

His body still pressed against me, his weapon at my throat, we continued our "death march" now into the open space of my room. As we moved toward the bed, he whispered what was to become his murderous refrain: "I'm going to rape you."

He never raised his voice.

I heard the door click shut with a chilling finality. I noticed he did not secure the latch and chain, but that glimmer of hope quickly faded when with icy detachment, he glared at me and in a rasping tone ordered, "Take off your clothes." Horrified, I began pleading, "I'll give you anything, but I don't want to do that."

By then he had released me. Uncontrollably shaking, I stood in front of him as he robbed me of my cash. With an eerie calm, he continued laying claim to my personal possessions, the next being my watch. As I looked at this endearing gift from Mama and Daddy on my college graduation day, I thought, "Oh no God, not my watch." I had never owned anything so lovely in my life. The memory of that special spring day quickened my hopes, but only for a moment.

As I unhooked the watch's clasp, I realized he would surely discover the love symbol of my life – my wedding ring. While removing my watch, I kept my arm close to my left side, all the while twisting the diamond hoping for a secure hiding place in the palm of my hand. As he grabbed the watch, my fist remained clinched.

Spotting my necklaces, he nodded his next demand, "Give those to me." All the while we never moved from between the beds. With the blade still pressed against my throat, he pushed me to the nightstand, yanked the phone from the wall and turned off the lights. The dark went deeper as he whispered for the second and final time, "Take off your clothes!" Again, I began to plead, "I don't want to do this." With the knife back in its death position, he shoved me closer to the bed. At this point I realized the tragedy that lay ahead. He was going to kill me. Yet facing this Satan, I knew no matter what, I would fight for life.

Trying not to draw his attention to my wedding band, I chose not to unbutton my blouse first. I took off my pumps, pantyhose and skirt. My underwear still covered me. That final protective shield. I paused as I saw my life flash in front of me. I had a loving husband, a caring family, and an idyllic life back in Statesboro. I removed my panties. "Get rid of the blouse." All that was left of my dignity was my bra. With no trace of emotion or vestige of compassion, his next order was, "Lay down on the bed and spread your legs."

Still filled with determination and resolve, I kept my legs closed trying to protect myself from the unimaginable nightmare I knew I was about to suffer.

Thoughts of that knife tormented me.

Where is it? In his hand? On the bed? When it reappears, will it be the last thing I ever see?

Next came a moment of desperate irony. With tears streaming down my face, I tried to become, in a way, like the monster who held me – oblivious, even indifferent, to the horror and inhumanity of his heinous invasion of my very soul. I turned my head toward the window and took in the twinkling lights of a vibrant city. But my mind returned to the awful reality at hand. As I think back now, I cannot imagine having such a moment of clarity in my captive state. My mind fell into unexplored territory. Was he going to use the weapon to mutilate my genital area? Was he going to use the phone cord to bind my hands or strangle me? Was the sexual violence going to be anal? Was he going to rip me apart? Was I going to endure this torment for hours? How violent was this going to be? Was he going to repeatedly rape me and then kill me?

The purity of my life in Statesboro had not prepared me to ask such terrible questions.

Then I cried out to the only One who could intervene.

"Lord, if you let me live, I will never miss a day of Church again."

"If you get me out of this, I will never sin again."

"Have mercy on me."

Were these empty promises and deal making? Was I offering my God a bargaining chip?

"Lord save me," I sobbed.

The sadist's next guttural command interrupted my petition: "Spread your legs."

Like the seismic waves that precede an earthquake, my body began to tremble. Now on his knees, with brutal strength he forced open my legs. With his hands on my inner thighs, I was captive in a pinned position. Then the invasion began. For the next five minutes, this demon slowly, methodically, branded that sacred part of my body with lasting scars, as the thrusts of his tongue seared my soul. I wish I could say it was all a blur. But it wasn't. I remember every second of those tortured minutes. It became an eternity of evil as this murderous stranger violated my body, heart, mind and soul, leaving wounds only the Eternal One could heal.

Suddenly there was a pause. A hesitation. The oral sex stopped. He rose from his crouched position. Trembling uncontrollably, I watched him walk to the bathroom and return with a dry washcloth.

What is he going to do? Gag me so I can't scream? Suffocate me? What else is a washcloth used for in sexual assault?

I had no idea, no clue. I never got the memo.

Mark, my life's partner, 200 miles away, had no way of knowing a monster was moving toward his wife again, with every intention of continuing to shatter her beloved promise "to have and to hold."

Traumatized by the degradation, my heart and brain joined forces and I thought as hard as I possibly could, *Okay Jenny Lynn. Who is smarter? This monster or you? Think. Think. Think hard. Think. Think. Be creative. Think. Think. Think.*

And in that second I decided I was going to survive this brutal assault. This beast from Satan. I moved to a place deep inside myself and drew upon every method of survival my mother Faye Sanders Martin had ever taught me. I remembered her accounts about enduring pain and suffering and the will to survive. With this innate ability and fortitude I had learned from the master survivor herself, I became like her with an inborn strength and my power came alive. With resolute conviction, I was a force not to be denied as I declared to my Maker that 939 would not be the end of my life.

Without hesitation, I began speaking slowly, in a tone void of emotion and doubt, "My boss will be here any minute. You can't do this." My voice grew stronger as I repeated the chant. "My boss is on his way to my room *right* now. He is going to find you." I now felt in control as I began firmly hurling threats at this monster. Do it Jenny Lynn. Even more defiantly, I repeated my warning, calculated and detached: "My boss Rodney is going to be here *any* second and find *you*."

Now nervous and flustered, the dark specter moved to the door, opened it slightly, listening for any threatening sounds. As the hallway's light streamed into the room, I knew my prayers had been heard. For there was the angel God had sent to stand in the perfect place, at the perfect time, just for me. The angel's eyes locked onto mine.

I was a woman gone mad, a caged animal, and what came out of the depths of my soul terrified even me. I screamed, "He's raping me ... help me ... he's going to kill me. He's raping me ... help me ... He's raping me ... He's raping me ... He's raping me. He's raping me. He's raping me." Like a raging brush fire, my pleas roared through the door into the hall as guests rushed from their rooms reacting with disbelief to the peals of horror filling the hallway. Fright enjoys its reality regardless of location and suddenly it took residence in the eyes of the black man, as with total abandon, this monster hurriedly pushed past the housekeeper, my angel, onto the emergency staircase.

Into the protective darkness of the city, this cruel invader vanished.

They never caught him.

3

Blueprint

Ideally, childhood should be a time of wide-eyed wonder and unbridled joy. It's never completely like that, of course, but for some of us, like my older sister Janna and me, it comes close. And for that, we can thank our parents. I've always believed I was born special and unique. To begin with, my mother blessed me with a built-in conversation starter, a name that would invite the immediate curiosity of most anyone who met me and ignite interesting dialogues with strangers who soon would become friends.

"Oh, were you named after that Swedish opera singer? Jenny Lynn, hmmm ... your name must come from the crib company. Did your Mama name you after a crib? Do you spell it with a J or a G?"

Mama also bequeathed me the genetic make-up of a genuine Southern girl, complete with the accent and personality to match the sugar in the sweet tea found only in the South. Face it folks; *I was a one of kind.*

We had a wonderful extended family on my mother's side of loving aunts, uncles, and cousins. On my father's side, I had a very special bond with my first cousin Jone Martin, my "noticer" and "listener." Four years my senior, she always influenced me with well timed and substantive advice. Also, my mother and father's best friends (and they had many) loved me deeply. It wasn't uncommon for our family to be at the homes of the Smiths, Howards and Courseys for fish fries, quail suppers, and barbecues where I was showered with attention and love.

Educated at a private school, Bulloch Academy, I learned from wonderful teachers, especially Miss Cissy Olliff, my 3rd grade mentor whose love and belief in me added to the healthy self-esteem already instilled by my parents and friends and established a powerful shield that would serve me well as I navigated my teenage years. Because I liked who I was, I escaped much of the self-consciousness and awkwardness that plague many teenagers. From the beginning, I was my own person, the one and only Jenny Lynn.

Our mother's profession was another factor that enabled Janna and me to be independent designers of our destiny. She was a busy attorney; thus we were atypical latch-key children in Woodlawn Terrace, a neighborhood where most mothers in the late '60s were stay-at-home moms. Mama was a partner in the law firm, Anderson and Sanders. It was sort of cool to have a mother who used her maiden name, Sanders, to practice law, and since she worked full-time, Janna and I developed a self-reliant mindset.

We spent summer days on our bicycles riding through the neighborhood, often making trips to the nearby Dairy Queen on Georgia Southern College's campus. It was not unheard of for us to "bike" five miles to the other Dairy Queen on the north side of town. Our community being a safe haven for adventurous outings, we enjoyed the freedom to explore every inch of Bulloch County without the safety net of a cell phone or a GPS to track our every move because while Mama and Daddy were at work, we had their trust. They were definitely not helicopter parents. We rarely even used the land line unless we wanted to call a friend about a spend-the-night party.

For you younger readers, that's what we did in "olden days." We had to actually spend time with our friends and communicate in complete sentences. We couldn't just sit up in our beds and text each other until three in the morning. Phones just weren't that important to us. They were a clunky, rotary dial apparatus used to share vital information and perhaps rang only four times a day. I remember always being excited when the phone rang.

Mama and Daddy's laid back parenting allowed us the freedom to bike to Johnson's Minute Mart for Coke Icees and Spree candy, to jump on the trampoline night and day, to ride our blue Honda 70 motorcycle sans helmet around the neighborhood, and chase the pest control "Skeeter Man" through Woodlawn Terrace. Truly, if I end up one day with some rare form of disease resulting in distorted horns protruding from my elbows, a friend at my funeral is likely to smile just a little, blame it on the thick choking fog emanating from the mosquito truck and say, "Lord knows Jenny Lynn loved to ride her bicycle behind that truck when she was little. Poor child didn't know it contained DDT and would cause her demise. Of course, she'd do it all over again, God bless her soul ... she was ecstatic in that fog."

An equally likely culprit could be all that water we drank straight from the pipes. We didn't drink bottled water unless we wanted to fill an empty coke bottle from a hose if we were outside and didn't want to take the time to go inside for a drink.

Ah, but my joy of the Skeeter man ended abruptly when a child carelessly rammed his bike into the truck's backside. Hearing the news, Mama and Daddy put a halt to my merriment ... no more Skeeter Man chasing. He didn't last much longer himself, not his job anyway, as DDT was eventually outlawed not long after. Truly it was a sad day in South Georgia when "skeeter sprayin'" stopped as armies of mosquitoes remained poised to ruin our outdoor events like back porch peanut boils, cookouts, and pond fishing. Yankees like to make fun of us and claim the pesky pest is the South's bird symbol. The joke's on them, though. Everybody knows it's the gnat.

Mama arrived at the office every morning at nine sharp, so the Martin children had no time to waste lollygagging. Therefore, Janna and I learned to be up and about doing something from the crib throughout childhood. We were constantly mapping strategies and designing solutions typical of childhood projects. For instance, each year we would eagerly orchestrate Mama and Daddy's February 6/7 birthdays. We were independent party planners, except for asking Mrs. Pat Thompson to carpool us by Cathryn's Bakery to pick up the birthday cake. We knew there was no way to transport Mom's surprise masterpiece by bicycle without dropping this white-iced jewel on Highway 67.

Our independent childhood taught us one important aptitude – quick thinking on our feet. Little did I know this skill would prove vital to my surviving 939. Like all working moms, ours often expressed regrets about not being home with us. But Janna and I always assured our mother we felt completely loved. Never short changed in that area of our lives, we began listening to her daily advice even more as we approached our teenage years. Still today, this able woman's wisdom serves Janna and me in every area of our lives. Her thoughtful comments offered stalwart advice: always be confident, committed, and determined to make a difference.

The good fortune that permeated my childhood seemed to follow me everywhere. I won hams at the County Fair, cakes at Halloween school carnivals, and turkeys raffled off at basketball games. Of course, by now you've probably guessed that I *have* tested a few boundaries in my time. Strong Southern girls know how to be ladies, but we also know how to have fun. I got through high school safe and sound, but in college, my extracurricular activities included lots of partying and late night carousing at local outlets such as Dingus Magee's, The Animal House and The Flame, all located near the college campus. Thursday night "Drink and Drowns" were especially popular. These raucous evenings would begin with specials for girls only. Then the guys, eager to socialize over buckets of beer, were allowed on the premises. It was a whirlwind of boozing followed by morning hangovers. Many nights my friends and I would be gathered in a cozy booth at Snooky's Restaurant at 2 a.m. enjoying club sandwiches, French fries and Cokes.

One memorable night during my sophomore year, I had an unfortunate experience that left a lifelong impression. I had transferred to the University of Georgia and was home for a weekend visit with my Phi Mu sisters at Georgia Southern. This regrettable incident took place when two of my sorority sisters and I borrowed my sister's car to visit several fraternity socials. I was the "designated driver," which in those days meant I was designated to drive drunk! Although DUI was a major infraction, it hadn't yet received the attention it would in the years to come. "Mothers against Drunk Driving" had yet to mount its worthy campaign to educate the public about this deadly practice, and Georgia had no "Click it" law, so many of us drove around in double jeopardy, intoxicated and sans seatbelts. In Janna's sporty, burgundy Grand Prix, we were making our way from the Sigma Chi's to the Kappa Sig's.

As I approached a downtown traffic light near

McDonald's, the car in front of me slammed on brakes, followed by a crash! Fortunately no one was injured. *Unfortunately* a police officer positioned at the intersection witnessed the accident. Within seconds, that dreaded duet of flashing blue lights and the "concerned" officer appeared at my window, requesting to see my license and asking "Miss Martin, have you been drinking?" I replied without hesitation, "Yes sir. We have been at the Sigma Chi house." He then asked, "Where are you going?" "To another fraternity party," I replied. All the while, an open wine bottle sat beside me in the console. I was toast.

He asked me to step from the car for a sobriety field test. I really didn't feel *too terribly* intoxicated. Neither crazy drunk nor totally without judgment. I followed his instructions and to my surprise, he handcuffed me and asked me to accompany him to his paddy wagon. The three-minute ride to the police department was an eternity. When we arrived at the station, the officer placed me in a stark white holding room, fingerprinted me, asked me a few more questions and invited me to breathe into the breathalyzer. I recall contemplating how I could exhale without releasing too many telltale vapors. So, Jenny Lynn puffed a quick breath followed by a furtive glance, hoping for a miracle. I blew a borderline illegal .10. In a matter of minutes, Jenny Lynn Martin had become a criminal!

It was after midnight when I was asked if I wanted to call someone. *Not really*, I thought. That doesn't sound like anything I remotely wanted to do, but I knew I had to face the music. I dialed home and of all times for Janna to be on the phone with her boyfriend, this was not the time – only she was. In the slammer, my one phone call wasted, I was doomed. Would I be stuck in jail all night? I had always blamed my sister for a lot of things, but this was too much. Of course, it didn't occur to me at the time that I'd just slightly altered the shape of her Grand Prix.

Fortunately I got another chance to call home. Holding the phone as it rang, I prayed, "Mother, please be the one to pick up, as my mom and not Judge Martin." I felt certain she would understand my plight. I could hear her saying, "Jenny Lynn, these things happen. Don't worry ... you'll get through this and we'll be there for you." Oh happy day! Mama answered the phone and gave me the shock of my life with her terse six-word response: "I'll send Hollis to get you." Sounded to me like I got the Judge.

Yikes. Talk about my world suddenly going dark. I think I felt the ground tremble as a tsunami named John Hollis Martin headed my way. It was only a 10-minute drive from our house to the slammer, but it seemed like another eternity as I braced for impact. After the arduous task of completing the numerous forms for my release, his only comment was, "Jenny Lynn, your Mama and I will talk about this with you in the morning."

In the morning? No ... not the morning. How about we touch on the highlights tonight and get through a little of this misery and mess right now?

No such luck. They went to their bedroom and I to mine for a sleepless night preparing to defend myself when the time came to face both "Judge Martins." I imagined various scenarios, reasoned explanations that would prompt understanding nods and reassuring hugs as we resolved to put this whole thing behind us. But I was haunted by the thought that I had never disappointed my parents in 19 years. The sobering truth is, however, I had made a really bad decision. Fortunately for me, no one was injured – no lives lost. Today I am reminded of how my fate could have been much different when I hear the news of how "one more for the road" is often the cause of tragedy. Daddy, always the stoic one, implanted his firmness in Janna and me as to what I now know was his design of love. A man of few words, Hollis Martin knew when to deliver "those few words." He had a special way of shaping his thoughts with precision and wisdom. And after that morning session with him, his caring and loving ways confirmed right from wrong, and I can assure you I never got behind a wheel drunk again. He was a good man, who at the young age of 59, lost a 12-month battle with cancer.

When I transferred back to Georgia Southern College to begin my junior year, a sense of self-discovery began to crystallize. In moments of reflection, we come to know ourselves better and to live with intention instead of merely letting life happen to us. Some are masters of their destiny; others are mastered by destiny. One afternoon at the library as I scanned the college's catalog, I had an epiphany. The majors and course descriptions offered by the Communication Arts Department piqued my interest. Broadcasting especially intrigued me.

Research shows fear of public speaking ranks as high as fear of death for many people. Not for Jenny Lynn! Speaking to a crowd has always come naturally for me. I'm as at ease as the most accomplished politician – only a whole lot more honest. When I was ten, Mrs. Cone, our 4th grade teacher at Bulloch Academy, had us prepare a speech on the personality and distinctness of a city and state. We chose our locations by drawing a slip of paper from a hat she passed around. Imagine my excitement when I looked down and saw New York, New York. I was thrilled beyond words. Big city lights, Broadway, swarms of yellow taxis, and throngs of the most interesting people in the world, the city that never sleeps – the perfect ingredients for a Jenny Lynn special!

I knew nothing about that horizon city, simply because I had yet to travel. But ah, Jenny Lynn knew instinctively she had struck gold with the "draw." I located the address for the NYC Chamber of Commerce and wrote a letter of introduction requesting materials to compose my report. Within a few days, a large packet of pamphlets and brochures arrived, complementing all my needs. It's nice to remember we once lived in a time when folks actually sat at desks, opened envelopes, and answered such requests.

I poured over the material and developed an outline for my presentation. As I moved my note cards to a selected chronology, I arrived at the *Pièce de résistance*: my speech, the time for me to shine! So I did what most 10 year olds would do: I practiced in front of the mirror. I knew I needed to memorize both the material and my delivery if I was to be my best. By the time the teacher had worked alphabetically to the M's, I had watched most of my classmates turn beet red, twitch, sweat profusely, and stammer out halting, monotone, barely audible "oratories." When the day came and Mrs. Cone called on me, I was more than prepared. Cool as a cucumber. My delivery was a finely tuned symphony, complete with well-timed pauses, inspired gestures, and lilting intonation. When I finished, the class erupted in cheers. By gosh, I was born to be a public speaker!

My experiences in the high school drama club only enhanced my love for the spotlight. I enjoyed every moment with never a hint of stage fright. I remember Mom's telling me, "You're a natural, Jenny Lynn. It's a gift."

With her praise resonating in my mind, I felt a surge of

confidence as I read about the introductory broadcasting courses students took before deciding to focus on either production or talent. I knew immediately which one I would choose: Cue the lights and camera. All the way from her auspicious 4th grade debut, "Here is Jenny Lynn Anderson with your six o'clock news ..."

"Good evening. It has been confirmed ..."

Oh, wow, my path to stardom lay ahead of me smooth and uncluttered. *Yeah, right.*

With grand plans to move through my major courses, graduate, and find those lights, set and teleprompter, I registered for "Introduction to Broadcasting." It might as well have been called "Introduction to Reality." Somehow I managed to stay awake as our professor spent the first two weeks lecturing on the history of broadcasting. Then, finally in the third week, he gave us our first major assignment: to write a news story and assimilate it into a two-minute "on the air" pitch. *Right down this girl's alley. Let's have at it.*

And have at it he did when I finished my tight two minutes. I returned to my desk, poised and prepared for his review. As far as I was concerned I had met the challenge: sharp copy, good eye contact and convincing content. Quiet reigned as he gathered his notes and walked to the front of the room. Turning, he said simply, "Jenny Lynn, your Southern dialect is so heavy; you'll never make it out there in the cut throat world of broadcasting."

I was crushed. And so was my dream due to the heavy Southern accent I had carefully crafted by my listening to Mom, Dad, friends and neighbors, and one certain classmate, Jessica Johnston, whom I loved dearly my whole life. We were inseparable, spending countless hours together. I do remember her being kidded about her twang, a drawl like none other. Now as I sat midst my shattered dream with the starkness of the instructor's comment ringing in my ears, should I blame dear Jessica for this moment? Probably about as much as I should've blamed Janna for being on the phone the night of my "unfortunate incarceration."

As I walked from class, a bit forlorn, it came back to me that just maybe the 'script was in the sand' when during an earlier speech class, we were positioned in the center of an auditorium stage and invited to recite, "The rain in Spain falls mainly on the plain." Nine simple words. Not hardly. My "a's" sounded like "rai-un" in "spa-un" falls "mai-un-ly" in the "plai-un." A look of disbelief filled the face of my professor. Over and over, he worked on my recitation with this one line. Endlessly he illustrated how to enunciate to his satisfaction. The poor soul suffered the entire quarter as he tried desperately to transform this drawling Eliza Doolittle. I know he must have given me a "B" for guts and effort. As I walked into the sunset, I remained Jenny Lynn with her Southern belle elocution.

I knew the broadcasting professor was right. A new ray of sunshine chased away that dark cloud, though, when my sorority sister Joy Hardin, a Public Relations major, told me about this field. It sounded intriguing. Her description of this work seemed to be another chance to follow my dream. I chose Public Relations as my new major and life's work and have never looked back.

With a strong foundation from middle school and high school under the tutelage of Tom McElheny, my English teacher, I had been exposed to major sentence diagramming, poetry, Greek mythology, and every grammar rule imaginable. He created a magical, perfect scenario for learning. "Mr. Mc," as we lovingly called him, was a gift from heaven to all of us at Bulloch Academy who had the opportunity to learn under this master of the English Language. Similarly to how God breathes the Holy Spirit into us, Tom McElheny breathed the beauty and majesty of words, grammar rules, spelling, and love of literature into our hearts and minds.

Thus, I approached my initial journalism class with verve and conviction. My B+ grade point average as a high school and college student shifted when I moved into Public Relations. Drum roll please ... I became a straight A student.

As though I had been placed on this planet with a Public Relations degree behind my name, I attended classes, immediately comprehending the depth of the profession and the impact it could have on the bottom line of a business. Armed with a solid dose of common sense and a keen, intuitive feel for people's reaction to written and oral language, I did well in courses involving PR planning and execution.

We all have those sea change moments that redirect the course of our lives forever, some of them beautiful and serendipitous, others not so much, of course, but more on that later.

A guest lecturer to my journalism class proved to be one such pivotal influence during my senior year. Diane DeCesare, sophisticated and professional, spoke to us about how important it was for students to work on portfolios containing writing samples for potential employers to review. I remember thinking, "What the heck is a portfolio?" She spoke about her position as Public Relations Director of Willingway Hospital, a world renowned drug and alcohol recovery facility in Statesboro.

I recall looking around during her speech at my classmates and experiencing a moment of undeniable clarity:

We are all a bunch of brown Tootsie Rolls, the same size, packaged in the same wrapper. How do I become that one unforgettable Tootsie Roll?

Forrest Gump was only partly right. Life may be like a box of chocolates, but sometimes you know exactly what you're getting because every piece is just the same. So you just reach in and grab. I didn't want to take that kind of chance. Anonymity just didn't sit well on Jenny Lynn. Suddenly I had an idea. I would introduce myself to Ms. DeCesare after class and inquire about a job. I knew working with this PR veteran would set me apart. I would be a One Hundred Thousand Dollar Bar midst a chocolate sea of Tootsie Rolls. They say it's better to be lucky than good. For sure, luck was on my side the day I visited Diane. She offered me a part time job as her assistant, and our coming together had God's imprint all over it. We became kindred spirits during those two wonderful years of our working together.

In 1985, before I landed my first real job in public relations at the Georgia World Congress Center, I was awarded a senior internship at Lockheed-Georgia (Atlanta), a position considered the pinnacle of on-the-job training, and it certainly opened doors for me when I began my job search. So much of what I had learned from Diane came directly into play at Lockheed where I assisted Roy Simmons, Director of Community Affairs. We designed and developed conferences ranging from in-house staff meetings to major visits from international business executives and potential Lockheed clients. Additionally, I learned how to develop tours for visitors to experience a first class look at this 4.2 million square foot facility and its 8,400 engineers and technicians. As a dedicated intern enjoying the challenges of working with Mr. Simmons, I became aware this was a significant time of recovery for Lockheed based on the Pentagon's decision to award a major contract for the construction of 50 C-5B Galaxies, a large military transport aircraft.

To be perfectly honest, the most daunting challenge I faced at Lockheed was learning to drive in Atlanta traffic. Until the day I arrived in the capital city to begin my internship, this girl had yet to experience such a maddening race of metal on wheels. I'm here to tell you, I-75 ain't no country road. During those early days of my internship, little did Mr. Simmons and his PR Director Everett Hayes – relaxed while chatting in the backseat – suspect the mortal danger they were in. Their chauffeur, the ordinarily unflappable Jenny Lynn Martin, did her best to deliver them safely to meetings in downtown Atlanta. Traumatic, yes, nerve racking, yes, but in that deliverance I gained precious experience that paid dividends as I battled harebrained drivers every day en route to the World Congress Center.

On the last day of my internship, loaded with farewell gifts, I hopped in my Nissan 200SX and floored it. With confidence and skill, I began weaving smoothly down the interstate. For certain, Jenny Lynn had learned how to wheel and deal in more ways than one.

4

The Rock

From the moment I met Mark Hudson Anderson, I knew he was solid as a rock. As our relationship developed, my independent nature complemented his solid demeanor. Needless to say, Mark immediately sensed the healthy dose of optimism in my genetic code, which was balanced with a sensible measure of caution, characteristic of Mom's side of the family. How often have I heard my Mom say, "Jenny Lynn ... are you sure you've considered what this might mean to you?" Mark brought some of that same measured outlook to our marriage, which for 25 years has been graciously balanced with give and take.

Mark entered the dating picture in the fall of 1983, when my Phi Mu sorority hosted a pledge dance and costume party to coincide with Halloween weekend. At that time, I was not involved with a "steady" and needed a date. My college roommates, Jill Mock and Elizabeth Anderson, pulled out a few fraternity composites and asked, "Why don't we take a look at these and see if we can find Jenny Lynn a really cute guy?" Qualifications: fun and easy on the eye. I was pondering the Alpha Tau Omegas as I came across Mark's photo. "Hey, how about Mark Anderson?" I posed. I knew him from those rare occasions I attended church. He was always there faithfully with his family. After this extensive research, I was confident enough about Mark to anoint him the "one." So I picked up the phone, called, and when he answered, I said, "Mark, hey, this is Jenny Lynn Martin," to which he responded with dead silence, what we've come to call "crickets." "This is a bit awkward," I mused. Definitely not used to such inexplicable indifference, I took the plunge and broke the silence with my well-known effervescent manner: "I was wondering if you'd be interested in going to the Phi Mu dance with me this weekend?"

Well, this is going great, another pause. Did he hear my name right? Yep, this guy's definitely laid back. Surely that's it. I'll bet he's holding the phone to his chest and mouthing to his roommates that it's Jenny Lynn Martin asking him for a date.

Well, I guess his roommates gave me the thumbs up, something like "Phi Mu ... hell yeah ... they throw a great party" because, after that second pregnant pause, he accepted my invitation.

When Mark arrived that Friday night, we slipped into our costumes – a pair of washing machine boxes I painted to look like gambling dice. As we approached his blue Chevette, it dawned on me there was no way we could squeeze into the compact wearing our outfits. With that, we tossed the boxes in the back and headed out. Sometime during the evening with the sounds of the Gap Band's "Burn Rubber on Me" blaring across Legends, a favorite watering hole, Mark turned to me and yelled, "Jenny Lynn, why are your nostril hairs so white?" I suddenly realized that inhaling spray paint fumes had left me with an unsightly nasal cavity. We had a good laugh with no hint of embarrassment. Mark Anderson, carefree and nonjudgmental. Hmmm ... Jenny Lynn ... there may be some possibilities here. What a fun evening!

At that time in my life, however, I was happy with the

single scene and had no real desire for any semblance of a steady. Neither was he. I had enjoyed a "first love," Bob Hanberry, from middle school until the summer before I left for college, so I had spent a carefree first two years as a coed. I was foot loose and fancy free. As for Mark, he was simply having the time of his life and wasn't interested in settling down – no serious stuff. However, my Phi Mu big sister Kelli Mock and her boyfriend, Jeff Dell, Mark's roommate, insisted we join them for their weekend shenanigans. They always offered a smorgasbord of tantalizing possibilities: "Hey, how about a ride in Jeff's jeep, and by the way, we've got a keg in the back. We're cooking spaghetti. Let's all eat at Jeff and Mark's apartment." By spring, their matchmaking skills had proven successful, and Mark and I were officially dating.

Mark took me home to meet his family on Easter Sunday, 1984. There, in the back yard of this wonderful country setting, were my future in-laws, outlaws, cousins, aunts and uncles. What a humorous clan. They were united with quick wit, a wickedly funny sense of playfulness, constant joking and incessant tomfoolery. It was slap stick humor at its best with a touch of corniness. Mark's father, Jake, whose warm smile and loving heart bathed his surroundings with a radiance matching the summer sun, set the tone for those genial gatherings. This angel of a man truly touched all who came to know him in a very special way.

I discovered in Mark's family an abiding respect for one another. A multi-layered spirituality permeated every nook and cranny of their home life, and the consecrated walk of Mark's mother, Merle Godbee Anderson, provided her family and friends a shining witness to God's grace. Her faith could be compared to Rebekah of the Bible, a woman of great obedience. Mrs. Merle, strong in her conviction as a Christian, led her children to the Lord by example. Like Rebekah, she had a servant's heart. Naturally, then, they were people of prayer and possessed an overflowing compassion. The Anderson family blessed their community through their generous love for others. Mark, as my husband and father of our girls, continues to bless us with his pleasant blend of both his mom and dad, fun-loving, yet God-fearing.

5

Valley of Death

Horror and disbelief marked the hours following my sexual assault. When the dark figure fled from my room, I ran to the door and slammed it shut. Hands trembling, I barely could fasten the safety lock. I slid into a crouched position as if the weight of my body could prevent the evil from reentering my life. Midst my begging cries, I slowly became aware of the housekeeper outside the door calmly asking if I was okay. I couldn't answer. I couldn't speak. I had spent all my breath screaming and crying. Suddenly, voices of two hotel guests added to the chorus of those wanting to help.

While I remained frozen in terror, the trio continued their pleading, but to no avail. The door to Room 939 was the gateway to Hell, a world suddenly dark and dangerous. And *he* was out there. How many others roamed on the hunt to devour? Though it was the scene of my soul's destruction, it was safer for me to remain a naked heap on the floor. Finally I pushed up from the dark carpet, wrapped my pink robe around me and inched toward the door. I opened it slightly. That was the limit to my courage. One of the guests promised me he would stand by the door until help arrived. Slowly I moved to the bed, as I pulled my gown even tighter around me. Terror quickly turned into chaos as hotel security moved onto the scene and peppered me with questions. Too fast. Too quick. With my sodomized body covered only by a thin robe, I was unable to gain any semblance of composure.

I could muster only inaudible, incoherent replies to those interrogators looming around me. They all seemed like phantoms from a phantasmagorical netherworld.

Rodney entered the room overwhelmed, like a child taking those first halting steps into the haunted house at the local fair. That's what it was, really, a house of horrors, like those with the mirrors whose every reflection is a twisted distortion. Only this was not pretend, as the harsh, staccato bursts of my sobbing punctuated the grotesque scene confronting him. I remember Rodney's staring at me, recalling the poised and competent colleague who had left him only an hour earlier. What ungodly act had transformed her into a disjointed shadow, her radiant countenance now dark and shattered?

Had I been capable of speaking, the only explanation I could have offered would have been the one searing thought burned into my soul: In 15 minutes, this fiend had mutilated me with his hands and tongue. Two thousand years ago, a Lamb's blood had washed my soul clean, but on that night a devil's lie convinced me I had been damaged forever beyond repair – body, mind, and spirit. He had not touched the sacred part of me, my true self that was – and is – "hidden with Christ in God," but many painful years would pass before I would lay claim to that beautiful truth once again.

Scan to see the
CHARCOAL SKETCH

Use a QR Code Reader on
your mobile device

I immediately became obsessed with washing myself clean. I desperately wanted to be as pure and peaceful as when I had opened that door an hour earlier. But the veil of deception that had descended upon me convinced me that such cleanliness was not to be. I couldn't rid myself of the filth and impurity now imprisoning me.

Take a bath Jenny Lynn. Scrub this man's filth away.

Still trembling with fear, I locked the bathroom door, moved to the tub and wept. I couldn't get the water hot enough. How hot does it have to be to erase that kind of stain? "Make it scalding, God, hot enough to wash away every trace of that vile tongue." The trembling did not stop. Neither did the sobs hemorrhaging from my wounded soul.

Later, the hotel security guards returned with news they had apprehended a suspect and were holding him in their office. They asked if I would accompany them to identify the person of interest. The thought of facing my attacker both revolted and terrified me. But what other choice did I have? I wanted him imprisoned, immobilized forever, just as I believed I would be, eternally captive to the taint of Room 939. When I entered security, I encountered no police lineup like those in movies. No two-way mirror to shield my identity. It was a stark, white, nondescript room in the bowels of the hotel.

Standing only a few feet from him, I took one look and gasped incredulously, "You've got the wrong man." Suddenly, the suspect lunged at me and growled, "You fucking bitch ... I didn't do this to you!" My God! My once idyllic world was being shattered like pictures ripped from the walls of a home in the throes of a violent earthquake. As security quickly whisked me across the parking deck to the elevator, I felt nothing could protect me from falling prey to this diabolic force that now imprisoned me.

When I returned to 939, I was stunned by the overwhelming glare of yellow tape, a stark reminder that an impassable boundary now separated me from my old life. I stood there a bruised, wounded, and crippled Jenny Lynn Anderson, who just 60 minutes earlier was checking her makeup and headed for dinner.

Finally officers from the Atlanta Police Department arrived and took me to the Sex Crime Unit. I recall being shocked at the words "Sex Crime Unit." Jenny Lynn Anderson here? Of all places, a sex crime unit? And as a victim? But there I was – in an alien world I would never have chosen to visit. The interrogation and probe into the events, timeline, and details lasted until three in the morning. I had no physical wounds – not even a nick. In a cruelly ironic way, I wanted some kind of obvious, physical evidence so I could scream, "Look, see this place on my neck. This is what he did to me. See ... it's right here. See, see ... this is the mark!" But I was left with nothing tangible to show. The real, unalterable damage was to my soul. We've all heard the expression, "bare your soul," but really how can others ever really see into that sacred realm and understand? Even those who love us and know us best reach a point beyond which only God can travel. So, there was nothing to "eye ball."

The police detective asked incisive questions, demanding distinct details, and he kept using a term that seemed to accuse me instead of my perpetrator: alleged – "alleged sexual assault," "alleged robbery." There was nothing "alleged" about what had happened in 939. When the probing finally ended, he asked if there was someone I could call.

The thought of having to call Mark in the middle of the night and tell him about the attack seared every cell of my mind. Such bulletins are devastating. It would discharge open wounds to his soul as he too became the demon's second victim. When the detective handed the black phone to me, the weight of the receiver and the call I was about to make overwhelmed me. How do you tell your husband you have been held at knife point, robbed, and given the choice of sex or death? How do you tell your husband you surrendered to sex for a chance to live? How do you tell your husband how it feels to have a stranger demand that you take off your clothes? How do you tell your husband you have been sodomized? How do you tell your husband you are no longer the woman he married?

There are no answers to such questions. There is no "how" to delivering a message like that. Nevertheless, with those thoughts haunting me, I wrestled with what I should say.

Jenny Lynn, how in the world are you going to begin this conversation? Honey ... I know it's the middle of the night. No. I haven't been in a wreck. No, I didn't get another DUI. Nothing so simple as that. No fender bender. No, I'm not sick. Long pause. Deep breath.

I have no idea what I actually said when Mark answered. I only remember talking to him in an uncharacteristically quiet tone as if somehow this would lessen the impact of the news. With his calm nature – the only soothing part of that night – Mark assured me, "Jenny Lynn, I'll call your Mom and we'll be leaving right away." Too traumatized to return to the hotel, I asked the police to call my collegiate Phi Mu big sister Kelli Mock Heartsill and tell her what had happened. Kelli arrived at the police station, shocked, confused and still short on details. Later at Kelli's, I took another long bath and did nothing but weep those few hours before daybreak. I couldn't close my eyes for fear the maniac could return at any moment. Because of a major work commitment the next morning, Kelli was unable to stay with me, so still concerned for my frightened condition, she did all she could to keep me calm as we drove to the home of Sandra Thackston Paris, another childhood friend of mine.

When Mark and Mama arrived at Sandra's, they were surprised to find Atlanta TV satellite news vans parked everywhere. In the early morning hours, my grief had turned to anger, and I had become unraveled over the ludicrous thought that I, a professional woman on a routine business trip, had overnight become a crime statistic. It infuriated me. For a moment, the old, spunky, Jenny Lynn returned – but only for a moment.

I had left the Georgia World Congress Center public relations post only weeks earlier, so many of the Atlanta broadcast journalists were close friends and colleagues. If I called, their response would be, "Hey Jenny Lynn. What's up?" I had cultivated both professional relationships and friendships with them during my years at the Congress Center and Georgia Dome. They would regularly contact me to reach the myriad of CEOs, dignitaries, and celebrities scheduled for an Atlanta convention or trade show. Day in and day out, as I coordinated media relations, they would ask for their "PR workhorse" to help them report the story. I loved every minute of the action.

So, the morning after the assault, I called the Atlanta NBC, ABC and CBS affiliates and contacted my friends in the newsrooms. Each of them was shocked by the incident. Two of the stations immediately dispatched crews. Upon their arrival, I sat in Sandra's living room and recounted my story of horror in complete detail and expressed my fear that when the segment "aired," the assailant might be able to see my face again. The reporters agreed to shadow my profile and distort my voice to maintain my anonymity.

My mind still totally dismembered, the journalist in me came alive as I assured viewers how such unimaginable invasions can happen regardless of time or place. Even in an apparently safe environment, the worst can happen. My poise and competence in telling the story were short lived, however. When the crews packed up and left, I felt myself plummeting once again into the abyss that had swallowed my old life.

When Mother arrived at Sandra's home and took in this press conference environment and her daughter's apparent composure, her judicial mind made a quick and accurate assessment. She questioned my decision to contact the news media. Her stern caution was delivered as a loving Mother as well as a learned judge – instincts to protect and care for me. Based on her reaction coming from a lifetime of wise counsel, I knew there would be no further contacts with the media. So, I canceled the third TV interview. The Atlanta press continued to call me even after I returned to Statesboro, but I declined each request, now convinced the ugly truth must remain unreported. It should be as if I had never crossed the threshold of Room 939. In the span of twelve hours, I became the keeper of a secret instead of a herald, warning her people of unimaginable dangers.

Needless to say, when Mark drove me to the hotel to retrieve my car to head home, I dreaded returning to the scene of my undoing. The structure loomed like a grinning specter as we approached, so I chose not to look. My eyes were swollen nearly shut from 14 hours of constant sobbing. This near blindness was a blessing, one of God's merciful graces granted me as this vicious narrative continued to unfold.

Mark turned to me and asked softly, "Jenny Lynn, do you want to ride home with me or your Mom?" Dazed and confused like a beaten, helpless animal, I could muster no response. Without a word, I crawled into the passenger seat beside Mama. I was undone. Like a battered rag doll, exiled to that corner of the universe reserved for the no longer useful, the indomitable Jenny Lynn Anderson headed down I-75 to a life of captivity in a world void of light and joy.

The handling of the crime scene in Room 939 should be a "How Not To" chapter in a Criminal Justice textbook. In those crucial moments following my invasion I was completely numb. Hysterical. Traumatized. Terrorized. Unable to think rationally, I remained unaware that no authorities had been there to make sure nothing was touched until the room could be swept for evidence.

Even worse, in that unfortunate void, no one stopped me from taking the bath that washed away vital DNA evidence. Because no one had cordoned off the crime scene, hotel guards and onlookers contaminated the room with fingerprints and heel marks. No one bagged my clothes and underwear for the necessary forensic evidence. And finally, no one took me to the emergency room for the required medical examination. In other words, within 180 minutes, I was victim twice: of the dark invader and of the hotel security's incompetence.

Sadly, too many cases like mine go unsolved due to this kind of carelessness that wastes the opportunity to gather vital evidence left by a perpetrator. Keep in mind the knife was at my throat at 8:00 p.m., but it would be midnight before the Atlanta Police Department questioned me about the details of my tragedy. I wish I could say I felt relieved when this process began, but both the authorities and I knew that by then it was too late. No DNA.

At some point during those jumbled hours in that stark, sterile police precinct, I must have grasped that fact – and along with it the hellish realization he would never be caught. His glowering, arrogant visage and raspy voice would haunt my every waking and slumbering moment. For the next 20 years, fear would become as much a part of me as had joy and optimism before that night.

As Mother drove down I-75 toward home, the only sign of life in her daughter was uncontrollable flinching and involuntary spasms of terror as flashbacks from Room 939 tormented her. Existing somewhere in netherworld between consciousness and elusive rest, I would emit sounds unrecognizable even to myself, as if trying to exorcise the demon who rode with us. At some point during the ride, midst the agonizing surrealism that engulfed me, as had happened intermittently during the previous few hours, another realization crystallized in my mind. With that I turned to the one person who had always loved me unconditionally and said, "Mama, there's something terribly wrong with me. I'm going to need help."

Southeast Georgia became an arctic landscape as my feelings froze into a protective, yet involuntary numbness. Hollow-eyed and hollow-hearted, I trudged through those initial days back home painfully aware of the eternal burden I would bear everywhere I went, the belief I had been tainted and would forever be "damaged goods."

The cruelty continued when Mama drove me to Bulloch Memorial Hospital on Saturday morning to be examined by Dr. Oscar Jackson, an Ob/Gyn. When Mama and I arrived, the Emergency Room receptionist asked casually what brought me out on such a cold, Saturday morning. *I wanted to say stomach virus. How about fever due to flu? No, even better, I clumsily fell down a flight of stairs and think I have a slight head injury.*

But the truth is I had suffered a spiritual heart attack and it had killed my soul. I answered by looking her straight in the eye and quietly responded, "I was sexually assaulted and I need to be examined." There ... it's out in the open for all the world to know and hear! I have added another entry to my resume. I have been sodomized. I am now labeled. *Jenny Lynn Anderson, sexual assault victim.* I hated these harsh words now defining me.

Having completed the necessary forms, I was then led into a chamber of sterile equipment and spectrum of blinding lights. Was this to be my life from now on? Clinical environments where I would face a never-ending series of inquisitions? I stood there taking it all in when suddenly my eyes fell upon the stirrups. Realizing this was not a routine checkup, I asked myself, "Can I really do this?" Then came the dreaded questions.

"How old were you when you began menstruating?"

Twelve.

"Have your periods been regular?"

Yes.

"Have you ever been pregnant?"

No.

"What type of contraception do you currently use?"

Birth control pills.

"The date of your last period?"

Bathed in sadness, I thought, *"I don't know. I can hardly remember my last name right now. What does it even matter?*

The only thing I do know is 36 hours earlier I was a normal, happy woman."

My last period was 14 days ago.

"Was there any penetration?"

I paused before I answered, thinking, *Penetration?* Tears welled in my eyes. I really didn't want to share such details with anybody, not even the nurse. I wanted this exam to end. I wanted my life to end. Oh yeah ... it already had ...

Yes. His tongue.

"How about his penis?"

No.

I recounted all the details with her before Dr. Jackson came in to conduct the physical examination. My sexual invasion was still palpitating within me when Dr. Jackson, unaware of the harsh command I had been given the night before, gently asked me to spread my legs. Would the cruel ironies never end? Why did I have to hear those words again so soon? I hesitated, not sure I could go through with it. Sitting at the base of the examination table was a man in a white coat with a stethoscope hanging around his neck. A trusted authority figure. A healer. But, I no longer believed in healing. All I could hear was my voice pleading, "No, not again!" I spread my knees a few inches and immediately began trembling again. Aftershocks. My legs quivered as I positioned myself for Dr. Jackson to begin his examination. It was the cold intrusion of the speculum which almost pushed me to the edge of what little sanity I had left.

For female victims, the pelvic exam is an important and essential, yet humiliating procedure. Her most private vessel has to be entered and explored in order for needed treatment to take place. But at the moment when the cold steel of the speculum enters her vagina, it does not feel like help. It screams "hurt." And this time, it screamed "Invasion!" Dr. Jackson apologized repeatedly during the exam, but my bruised heart could not comprehend his kindness. My new world no longer included such virtues.

The cultures would be checked for gonorrhea, herpes, chlamydia, syphilis, a complete panel for infectious diseases. He took several samples, which would provide any damning evidence still lurking inside me. But I knew the truth. My incessant scrubbing had erased every vestige of Room 939. In the face of yet another invasive trauma, it seemed the only destination for my grieving soul would be death.

After the exam, Dr. Jackson spoke to me with concern, but his kind demeanor could not soften what he said. "Jenny Lynn, because of the assault, we will need to do an HIV test, which we will repeat in several months."

Looking back, I don't know how I absorbed that blow. I had never considered I could be HIV positive. I went to Atlanta a perfectly healthy young woman and returned home with the harsh possibility I could be infected with a sexually transmissible virus. I waited and wondered if those "flu-like" symptoms would attack my body. Any time I experienced a chill, rash or night sweat, I wondered if the disease had taken residence in me and would end my life.

Upon leaving the hospital that morning, for some insane reason, I guess a futile attempt to reclaim some semblance of normalcy, my mother and I went straight to the Statesboro Mall as if to say, "See Jenny Lynn ...

Belk still has 20% off just like last week." But the hits just kept coming. Mama and I were walking out of JC Penney when an elderly woman approached us and "inquired" of Mama in a gossipy, hushed tone about "one of your daughters who had been assaulted." It was another out of body experience. Had I died in 939? Had I actually gone to Hell? Were all these normal looking people really devils there to torment me for eternity? Was everyone but Mama and me in on the joke? Here, this inconsiderate woman was talking about me as if I weren't standing right there. I remember thinking, *Let's just haul out the dirty laundry and air it in front of the department store for the whole world to see and touch.* I was livid at this woman's thoughtless inquiry. In my honest opinion, people are too often inconsiderate in their expressions to someone dealing with tragedy. Of all the condolences I was subject to, this is the one that took the cake as a lady gently held my hand, patted it, and said, "This too shall pass."

Well, if so, when? Tell me the date, time and place and I'll pencil it in my calendar.

Sarcasm didn't sit well on Jenny Lynn, but really, who was Jenny Lynn now? Did she still exist?

The woman might have offered a genuine expression of concern: "Faye, I heard the news about your daughter. Please know I have been thinking about your family and will pray for you." Or, "Faye, I heard your daughter was hurt terribly. I will always be there for you and your family."

Actually, the most compassionate thing she could have said would have been a quick, passing "Hey, y'all taking in the Saturday sales, too?" or something equally nondescript. Even kind words have their time and place. We can't live as if these things didn't really happen, but sometimes, the elephant in the room needs to go unmentioned. I had been injured beyond belief, but that man had hurt my precious Mother, too. When your child gets hurt, your heart aches in indescribable ways. Believe me when I say my mother, born during the Depression, had faced and overcome heartrending and unbelievable challenges in her life. But even those long, tough trials had not prepared her for this land mine, the defamation of her daughter.

6

Spiritual Awakening

"It is more blessed to give than to receive." Acts 20:35

    I first became aware of God as a nine-year-old in the Statesboro Primitive Baptist Church's Primary Sunday School Class. I was drawn to Mrs. Frieda Beasley, my first Sunday School teacher, who filled my heart with joy and love for the Lord. I can still see Mrs. Beasley's snow white hair, horned rimmed glasses and smiling countenance as she led us to her Savior each Sunday by sharing His story. She was simply wonderful in making certain we knew her Father was real, loving and accepting. She affirmed her faith at the close of each class by leading us in singing "God loves the little children of the world, red and yellow, black and white, they are precious in His sight." "Now remember, children," she would smile, "God is my best friend, and He can be yours too, if you believe."

    Little did I know how this kind lady's postscript would sustain me 20 years later during my nightmare in Room 939. However, like so many who grow up in the Church, especially in the South, I heard other messages that filled me with ambivalence and doubt. Our pastor, a powerful orator, scorched our congregation with sermons that contrasted sharply with Mrs. Beasley's soft symphony of love. Unlike Mrs. Beasley's Master, who offered unconditional love and support, the God of hellfire and brimstone I heard about in church petrified me, and I remember sitting in those pews confused and afraid. Many times, I looked into Mrs. Beasley's loving face wanting to ask, "Is our preacher talking about the same God you believe in?" I never asked the question, though, as she constantly reminded us that her Lord and ours is a Father of peace and understanding as described in Psalm 103:8: "*The Lord is compassionate and gracious, slow to anger, abounding in love.*" No flames in Mrs. Beasley's Sunday School Class. Whereas the pastor warned of God's judgment, she taught me about His mercy. I definitely found the latter more comforting.

But truthfully, when church let out, and the sun filled me with warmth as I skipped across the portico to Mama's car, images of damnation and judgment, thoughts of God's harsh punishment daunted me. A deep strain of legalism and "salvation by works" characterizes much of Southern Christianity, at times making believers feel stained with guilt instead of forgiven by grace. Just how good did I have to be to avoid those eternal fires? Only later did I learn of God's grace and that only Christ could make me truly righteous.

Remembering the dichotomy of my Sunday School teaching and Morning Worship preaching, as I became a mother of two girls, I guided Morgan and Allison through their childhood years with stories of our gracious, yet expectant Savior. I didn't want their spiritual awakening to be jumbled and confused by conflicting messages, and I knew that, at this stage of their lives, they needed to hear more about grace than about punishment. I am certain my pastor considered his "raising the roof" offerings right on target. But, as an eight year old, that's just what I felt like: a target. Our Lord talked a lot about hell, but he addressed His warnings to those who denied the truth right before their eyes, not to those eagerly seeking the Way and the Truth. As recorded in John's Gospel, Jesus, as he neared his death, prayed that all who believe in Him would be granted an astonishing privilege: adoption into the eternal fellowship of the Holy Trinity. He prayed *"that all of them [us] may be one, Father, just as you are in me and I am in you. May they also be in us"* (John 17:21). Everything in the universe centers on relationships, which are the key to all existence. God created us to share in an eternal dance of love and fellowship – to delight in Him and in each other. That's why relationships truly enrich our lives when they work and hurt so badly when they go wrong. And that is perhaps the gravest wound I suffered in Room 939. Violating another human like that man did me constitutes the very antithesis of God's purpose in creation. Evil cannot create; it can only attempt to destroy the good and the beautiful. The result is separation – from others, from oneself, and ultimately from God. The man who molested me wanted to drag me into the hell of isolation, and he almost succeeded. I did indeed go to a dark, desolate, lonely place, even when among loving family and friends. It is a long climb back to restoration, but Mrs. Beasley's Master never let go of me.

Still today, I believe the "teaching" and the "preaching" are too often imbalanced. I don't mean to condemn or judge, but I find the words of that wonderful old-fashioned hymn more revealing of God's character:

"Softly and tenderly, Jesus is calling ... calling to you and to me ..."

And so I chose to ingrain that message into my daughters as they awoke spiritually. That's what those Sunday mornings in Mrs. Beasley's class taught me, and, as a mother, I have believed and lived out that truth. I want Morgan and Allison to know how much God loves them. Of course, they must also understand that they must obey Him and that disobedience does have consequences. Even then, however, He deals with us much like Mama and Daddy did Janna and me when we veered off the "straight and narrow" – only on rare occasions, of course. The morning after my DUI, for example, wasn't a pleasant experience, but at no time did they make me think they loved or respected me less because of my mistake. Kids with parents like that find it much easier to believe God loves them and desires to bless them above all else.

I don't want Morgan and Allison to lose sight of these comforting truths, even when they struggle. I knew He would always be with me, but as that "dark night of the soul" descended upon me in that hotel corridor, I began to doubt all those Sunday School lessons Mrs. Beasley had taught me. If God existed at all, maybe He really was like the angry one my childhood pastor told us about. My despair obscured what I knew deep in my heart to be true. The apostle Paul urged the church at Corinth to hold fast to "faith, hope, and love," but for a time at least, faith and hope became strangers to me.

As of this writing, 21 years have passed, and I continue to heal. I say "continue" because, although my assailant's knife never cut me physically, the sheer, raw ugliness of that night pierced places in me that only God can see. Those scars that serve as reminders of healing often mask those places where we are most vulnerable. Now and then, the commonplace daily occurrence stabs one of those tender spots, and a sudden burst of hemorrhaging buckles my knees. God did not forsake me that night, and He has blessed me with a good life, but for a long time, I blamed Him for what happened to me. The stark, clinical atmosphere of the hotel security office, the cold formality of the police precinct, and the raw embarrassment of the hospital examination room back in Statesboro mirrored my inner landscape. I was empty inside, unable to feel anything but anger. Yes, I was surrounded by love from Mark, Mama and Janna. They propped me up and assured me that "in time, Jenny Lynn, the nightmare will fade and you will be able to feel safe as you fall asleep; you will be able to drive alone; you will be fine." For so long, I heard their words, thinking that's all they were – just words. Fear had shattered my faith and ability to trust. Although I felt blessed by all their love and support, I believed I had discovered an awful truth they just couldn't see:

But they don't understand. This world isn't safe! If it can happen once, it can happen again. And if it happened to me, it can happen to you and to anyone we love. Terror is everywhere, and it can pounce at anytime! Be on guard, Jenny Lynn. Be on guard all the time! If only my life could be the way it was before I opened that hotel door.

I felt like the speaker in Robert Frost's poem "Birches" who, when life turns dark, longs for the simple, carefree days of his childhood:

It's when I'm weary of considerations,
And life is too much like a pathless wood
Where your face burns and tickles with the cobwebs
Broken across it, and one eye is weeping
From a twig's having lashed across it open.

In the past 21 years, I have spent many a day in "pathless woods." I wept when a random comment or a news headline struck too close to home. A stranger approaching across a parking lot created moments that lashed across my soul and opened an old wound.

Today, Morgan is an advanced student at the University of Georgia, and Allison a rising soccer star in high school. Mark remains steadfast in his love for all of us. My mother and Janna offer me unwavering support, and I have a rich reservoir of good friends. But, I must deal with fear every day. I have learned its ways, however. I know when it lurks near, wanting to devour me. I am still on guard, but I am a strong, vigilant sentinel, aware of the enemy's tactics and armed with the knowledge that I am stronger than he is – and most importantly, that "Greater is He who is in me" than the one who would steal my peace.

So what does Jenny Lynn do as she remains equipped for the battle? I "put on the full armor of God," and I pray without ceasing – anywhere, anytime, in the grocery store, at the stop light, in the shower – that He will rescue me from these sudden ambushes. I know His love, and His grace, and His protection never cease either. With the psalmist, I affirm that *"Yea, though I walk through the valley of the shadow of death, I will fear no evil. For Thou art with me"* (Psalm 23:4).

Mark and I also nurture our faith and have always guided our girls to love the Lord by being active in the church. Admit it folks, going to church, singing hymns, tithing and saying "amen" now and then won't get us to heaven. Only God's grace does that. But being part of a church family is a vital part our Christian walk.

As I slowly healed and returned to the Lord, the Holy Spirit, the same Comforter that had come to live in that eight year old in Sunday School, gradually thawed my frozen feelings. So, eventually, I reached a point in my "re-growth" where I became able to commit myself to sharing His word, and I chose teaching Sunday School as a way to begin serving Him again. I explain to my 10-year-olds what God is all about and what He expects of us, how even at their age, they can represent His love by being good, doing their homework, and behaving for mom and dad. I call on my memories of wonderful Mrs. Beasley, and just like then, we read our story books and sing our songs.

"Jesus Loves Me This I know...for the Bible tells me so. Little Ones To Him Belong ..."

I find love and freedom during our weekly women's Bible study, and joy fills my heart while attending our Wednesday night youth activities.

As Sidney Poitier said the night he won the Oscar for his marvelous role in Lilies of the Field, "Folks, it has been a long way from there to here." I cannot think of a more appropriate closing to this visit called "Spiritual Awakenings" ... for indeed it has been a long way from there to here, and I am happy to report, though I gave up on Him, He never gave up on me, and each day I spend as a wife and mother, He continues to restore my soul.

7

Living, Loving, and Learning

During my teens, I began channeling my energies into interests more exotic than biking expeditions to unexplored parts of Bulloch County and trailing the "Skeeter Man." Inhaling those DDT vapors just didn't cut it anymore. During adolescence, the joy and wonder of a happy childhood become turbocharged with an electrifying infusion of hormones as bodies begin to blossom and eyes begin to open. Consequently, much that I had considered commonplace suddenly transformed into the extraordinary. As we grow older, our thoughts about certain people begin to, shall we say, evolve. Take boys for instance. One day, it's "Boys, ugh" or "Boys? They're okay, I guess, but I could never like them in *that* way." Then, it's a slight shift to "Well, maybe that way's not so disgusting after all." And a little later: "You know, he's really cute." Pretty soon, we decide we like them a lot, actually a *whole* lot.

Although girls remained my close companions and spend-the-night pals, boys began to be my favorite, at first not in a "boy likes girl" kind of way, but rather because they were simple creatures without the drama so prevalent among girls. They were easy to read, and I liked the uncomplicated nature of their friendship. No one fit that niche in my life better than Robby Williams. Nicknamed "Big Rob" by our peers, he remained Robby to me. I always thought the name "Big Rob" stripped him of his purity and goodness. But what could I do about this "tag"? High school nicknames stick tighter than river mud. Tenderhearted, he and I were often the ones to "tear up" when a teacher rebuked us or when a kid hurled a snide comment our way. Sticks and stones hurt less to some of us than do the pricks of hurtful words.

We were true soul mates. With similar work ethics, Robby and I usually earned the same grades – B's. He loved me like a sister, and he had my back, no matter the situation.

But the teenaged Jenny Lynn Martin soon took keen notice of what the hormonal onslaught had done to the boys surrounding her. Seemingly overnight, they became a strapping, good looking, All-American smorgasbord of freckles, blue eyes and blond hair, or brown eyes and wavy hair – yes, the ordinary had definitely transformed!

As our homogenous group moved fluidly into high school, our daily interactions invited seniors to become a part of our sophomoric lives. We thought we were ready for them; and we were. Within our small group came the beginning of an unannounced sexual awareness.

High school provided a steady stream of fun and excitement as weekend trips with our Headmaster to the North Carolina mountains, co-ed bus trips for football players and cheerleaders, barn parties and dances at friends' houses left little time for boredom.

Having come of age in the 1960s, many of them influenced by the permissive doctrine of pediatrician and author Dr. Benjamin Spock, parents in the '70s adopted a more lax attitude than had any generation in American history. Setting boundaries that strike a balance between strictness and leniency can be a real high wire act, but Daddy and Mama accomplished that task with their usual wisdom and good sense. Consequently, just as we had in those carefree days when Janna and I had biked around town, my friends and I had room to gradually, yet steadily make the transition from children into adults, always a perilous metamorphosis, especially given the romantic passions that began to waft about the halls of Bulloch Academy.

Of course, exploring relationships and intimacy is a natural rite of passage at this age. During this time of learning and growing, many couples, especially Janna and Robbie, Mark and Beth, Jessica and Brad, and many more, took the logical next step, going steady. Though public displays of affection were against school rules, it didn't exactly take a keen eye to spot the quick embraces and furtive kisses that took place behind closed doors and around corners.

Those smoldering embers, barely contained at school, ignited into full-blown flames at more opportune moments. Hay rides on freezing January nights became the scene of many a private (and some not so private) moments of passion. All in all, it was a magical time, when we came of age, thanks in part to what we considered our benighted parents. Now, of course, as the mother of two girls, I know that parents are never quite as ignorant as their kids think.

We returned from those hayrides, bodies covered with hay, hair all mussed, and convinced that our parents suspected we had done nothing more risqué than some innocent frolicking in the hay. Now, Jenny Lynn the mom knows just how much our parents weren't fooled. They knew they could trust us, though.

I've never shared details of the passion I felt for my first love, Bob Hanberry, powerful feelings that remain cherished memories stored in a special place in my heart. Every girl should have a first boyfriend like Bob. Our courtship laid the foundation for the mature approach I always took toward relationships and eventually my marriage to Mark. Bob and I remained pure through those magical teenage years. Although we never consummated our love, it was evident every day of our lives in unspoken words and mutual respect. Our belief in waiting until the wedding night always overshadowed our desire for each other.

Fortunately, the power of that love trumped an incident involving an unwarranted sexual experience that took place when I was 15 and remains with me to this day. Our family was spending the weekend at our coast house on Colonel's Island. While the adults were playing cards and having a grand time eating crabs and sipping cocktails, my friend Jessica and I begged one of Mom's and Dad's friends who lived near the coast for a cruise in his truck equipped with a CB radio, the rage of the 70s. We all had "handles." "Breaker, Breaker ... what's your 10-20 good buddy?"

With the three of us in the front seat, we headed to Half Moon Marina on a route that would allow us to pick up signals from truckers barreling down Interstate 95. Totally engrossed in "Breaker, Breaker" chatter, I suddenly felt a hand fondling my breast. Disbelief shocked me as I realized I was being taken advantage of by our 47-year-old family friend, who had always been a loving, trusted adult. The one who took us clam digging, crabbing, and allowed us one more loop as we water skied. My mother and father would no doubt have severed all relationships with this man had they ever found out about this unspeakable act. But they never knew. Like most girls violated in this way, I kept silent and realized membership in this sisters' society of secret keepers comes with a heavy price. It's called bondage.

8

War Zone

On Monday following the assault, the Atlanta Police Department called to inquire if I could return to Atlanta to meet with a forensic sketch artist who was to draw my invader's face. I knew without a doubt I would recall the details as the cruel lines of his features had besieged my every waking and sleeping second in the aftermath of those 72 hours. His full lips, chiseled cheek bones, fairly narrow nose, and steely eyes – a face completely void of human sympathy – loomed over the shoulder of everyone I met or around every corner I turned. I saw that malevolent leer in the most otherwise benign circumstances. It was as if he had never fled Room 939, but had instead become a specter that only I could see.

Still emotionally and physically drained, I told Mark, "There's no way under the sun I can make that three-hour drive." Fortunately, I didn't have to. The Mooney family, who owned Willingway Hospital, offered their corporate jet for Rodney and me to make the trip.

We left the next morning around nine, and by noon, the sketch artist showed me the results of our combined efforts. The picture was vividly real; it was as if the black man had come in to pose. Perhaps he had – in a way. As I rose to leave, I turned to the officer and said simply, "That's our man."

Later, as the plane climbed into the sky and I took in the vast expanse of Atlanta, a chilling thought punched me in the gut.

Jenny Lynn, he's still out there.

I felt an icy hand grip my heart, different and more threatening even than all the other alien emotions that had engulfed me. As I glanced longingly at my wrist where my graduation watch once rested, I was met with the face of a substitute timepiece, a talisman that could never erase the past few days or perhaps awaken me from my nightmare. Its hands moved in only one direction: forward – into an ominous future where danger and evil lurked, poised to destroy every sacred and safe place in my life.

Room 939 had shaken me to the deepest parts of my being. I became a shell of the sunny Jenny Lynn who saw problems as opportunities instead of obstacles, and who found something to like about most everyone she met. My world became an alien place, a pockmarked minefield, where every step could trigger tragedy, and even the most loving and encouraging of family and friends provided scant solace.

Within months, I learned I was suffering Post Traumatic Stress Disorder (PTSD). Hearing that verdict, I pored over every publication I could find in an effort to understand PTSD. In many ancient cultures, it was believed those who could name their demons could gain control of them. Maybe that was part of my motivation. I believe, too, that I found comfort in knowing I suffered from something with a medical name rather than from a soul indelibly stained by that man's tongue. She would need help, of course, but Jenny Lynn could fix this!

Immediately, I was overwhelmed by the history of this disorder. Ironically, its roots reach back to the cradle of Western Civilization, Ancient Greece, and to what for centuries was known strictly as a woman's affliction. The term "hysterical" stems from the Greek word for uterus: *hystera*. The Greeks believed the uterus was a sort of free-floating organ that migrated to different locations within the female body. If this nomadic bit of tissue ended up in the wrong place, it could, at least temporarily, cause the woman to become "emotionally distressed" – in a word, hysterical. For centuries medical "experts" thought people exhibiting symptoms for which there was no apparent physical cause suffered from one of three maladies: demon possession, some sort of brain injury invisible to the naked eye, or hysteria. And, only women could suffer from this latter malady, for only they had a uterus. Any man with similar mysterious symptoms surely suffered from an undetectable brain injury. All perfectly logical, yes?

Then, in the late 19th century, a major paradigm shift began to occur, due in large part to the work of Sigmund Freud, whose theories were initially met with derision, only to be validated during World War I. Originally a neurologist, Freud studied under Jean-Martin Charcot, a French neurologist who also practiced hypnosis. After observing patients whose symptoms, such as paralysis, would disappear while under hypnosis, Freud became convinced that some symptoms originated in what he called the subconscious mind – a repository of fears and inhibitions the conscious mind could not, or would not, acknowledge.

The medical profession received Freud's concepts with staunch skepticism because his hypothesis led to an inevitable – and absurd – conclusion: men could suffer from this affliction as well! He gained credence, however, during the war when soldiers began returning from the front exhibiting a variety of symptoms – paralysis, uncontrollable body tics and spasms, the inability to speak, incurable insomnia, and others – even though they had not been physically wounded. Initially puzzled, doctors soon concluded the soldiers' brains had been damaged by the tremendous concussions of exploding shells. In a word, they were said to be "shell-shocked," the origin of that familiar term. Still no such thing as a hysterical man!

But then soldiers who had never been to the front began to display the same symptoms, though clearly not "shell-shocked" or otherwise physically injured. Fear had paralyzed these poor men. They had been virtually scared to death. One could say they had literally been petrified. Consequently, medical science began to comprehend the power of the human mind – and of fear.

These were not exactly brand new discoveries. Even as far back as the early 1800s, military doctors had diagnosed soldiers returning from battle with "exhaustion" caused by their bodies' natural shock reaction to a most unnatural experience, combat. During this same period in England, victims of catastrophic railway accidents were said to suffer from "Railroad Hysteria." Survivors of the American Civil War suffered from what was called "soldier's heart," a reference to the frequency of arrhythmia, startled responses to unexpected stimuli and hyper-vigilance. More recently, World War II GI's returned to their families plagued with "combat fatigue," and in my generation, most of us knew or at least knew about a tormented veteran of the Vietnam War searching in vain for peace and restoration.

Readers familiar with the infamous World War II incident when General George C. Patton slapped the soldier suffering from "combat fatigue" know how slowly some antiquated ideas die. Consequently, even now, many think only the weak and cowardly – or the feminine, I guess – fall prey to this "illness." It was not until the early

1950s that the American Psychiatric Association defined PTSD as "stress response syndrome" brought on by "gross stress reaction." Still, that organization waited until 1980 to recognize PTSD as an official diagnosis and include it in the *Diagnostic and Statistical Manual of Mental Disorders* (DSM-III).

Today, the DSM-IV-TR defines post traumatic stress disorder as:

A. The person has been exposed to a traumatic event in which both of the following have been present:

(1) the person experienced, witnessed, or was confronted with an event or events that involved actual or threatened death or serious injury, or a threat to the physical integrity of self or others. (2) the person's response involved intense fear, helplessness, or horror.

B. The traumatic event is persistently experienced in one (or more) of the following ways:

(1) recurrent and intrusive distressing recollections of the event, including images, thoughts, or perceptions.

(2) recurrent distressing dreams of the event.

(3) acting or feeling as if the traumatic event were recurring (includes a sense of reliving the experience, illusions, hallucinations, and dissociative flashback episodes, including those that occur upon awakening or when intoxicated).

(4) intense psychological distress at exposure to internal or external cues that symbolize or resemble an aspect of the traumatic event.

(5) physiological reactivity on exposure to internal

or external cues that symbolize or resemble an aspect of the traumatic event.

C. Persistent avoidance of stimuli associated with the trauma and numbing of general responsiveness (not present before the trauma), as indicated by three (or more) of the following:

1) efforts to avoid thoughts, feelings, or conversations associated with the trauma

(2) efforts to avoid activities, places, or people that arouse recollections of the trauma

(3) inability to recall an important aspect of the trauma

(4) markedly diminished interest or participation in significant activities

(5) feeling of detachment or estrangement from others

(6) restricted range of affect (e.g., unable to have loving feelings)

(7) sense of a foreshortened future (e.g., does not expect to have a career, marriage, children, or a normal life span)

D. Persistent symptoms of increased arousal (not present before the trauma), as indicated by two (or more) of the following:

(1) difficulty falling or staying asleep

(2) irritability or outbursts of anger

(3) difficulty concentrating

(4) hyper-vigilance

(5) exaggerated startle response

E. Duration of the disturbance (symptoms in Criteria B, C, and D) is more than one month.

F. The disturbance causes clinically significant distress or impairment in social, occupational, or other important areas of functioning.

I have never experienced military combat, but I have been to war. The events in Room 939 represented the first salvo in a prolonged and exhausting conflict. I returned from Atlanta that day just as "war weary" and hyper-vigilant as the most traumatized veteran. Only my fight wasn't over. I was no longer fit for duty, but the landscape of my life had become a ravaged battlefield, littered with the corpses of my former idyllic existence. The child Jenny Lynn, wide-eyed and spontaneous; the newly-wed young professional with the limitless future; Jenny Lynn, the embodiment of the American dream, all seemed to fade away. Images of my lost self paraded in front of me as I sat in the chair in my den that became my bunker. They stopped to cast one last wistful glance good-bye before they faded to black – followed by a familiar, grinning, menacing visage who stood for a moment as if to say, "Look what I took from you. Take one last peek at what you'll never get back."

And there I sat, hunkered down in my den chair fortress, a Jenny Lynn I barely recognized, attempting to process just how disengaged I had become and how changed my world really was. I was a frightened soldier awaiting the enemy's next onslaught. Behind this hastily erected barricade, I clutched at some tenuous sense of safety.

But Jenny Lynn, just one chair? In the den? Yes, just one chair; it's a beginning. I can see the doorway from here, so nobody can sneak up on me. Any attack will be head on, and I'll be ready. I ... have ... got ... to be ready! I will be ready.

While my mind reeled from the shock and the lingering effects of PTSD, my sensory skills stood ready at DEFCON One, awaiting the attack I expected to come at any moment. An electric current of anxiety and fear surged through my body. I was like the child afraid of the monster under the bed or in the closet, for whom every "bump in the night" means a predator is about to pounce. But I was also angry, very, very angry, and a part of me would've welcomed a fight. Vengeance jostled with fear to gain the upper hand in my consciousness and sometimes won. My enemy, however, was a coward, and I knew that his kind never dared a frontal assault. He was a guerilla fighter; his chief tactic was the sneak attack on the defenseless, unsuspecting victim. So, I waited, alert to every gust of wind, or creaking floor, or fleeting shadow outside my window.

WW I soldiers spent months on end in muddy trenches, knowing that any moment a sniper's bullet could kill them. Most had watched others fall prey to an enemy they never saw, firing a shot they never heard. There were, however, more terrifying moments, those times when commanders issued the blood-curdling command to leave the trenches and charge across "no-man's land" into a hell of unspeakable horrors.

I had to give myself that same order. I had to go to work. Like those brave men, I had to show myself to a foe who could be anywhere, but I could barely make it from the kitchen to the carport. Its door posed a particularly difficult problem. *I had to actually open it.*

So I would run from the house through the garage, leap into my car, and immediately lock the doors. With the engine's power pulsating under my trembling hands, I backed into a world where flying bullets, artillery shells, and minefields awaited me in the form of strange (and familiar) faces, traffic lights that lingered for an eternity, cars that followed a little too closely, and a thousand other dangers that used to be ordinary parts of normal days. All the while, electricity sizzled through my body.

Back home at night, with Mark there to protect me, I felt no relief. Our bedroom, the place of our greatest intimacy, became just another outpost in the conflict, and Mark a conscripted soldier called to serve in my undeclared war. Afraid the dark figure could be lurking in my yard, I made Mark close and lock the bedroom door. He even offered to switch sides of the bed since I slept closest to the hallway. But that didn't help. His side faced the window.

Undressing, once a perfunctory task, exacerbated the nightmare. I would lock my bedroom door and move through my dressing area into the walk-in closet where finally I would begin taking off my clothes. This ritual went on for years as I wept while those haunting words, "take off your panties" echoed in that small chamber.

Those were the "normal" days I fought to endure and somehow managed. Then, at times, it was as if someone threw a switch, and panic would seize me without warning and churn my life into absolute chaos. Although I knew these attacks were inevitable, their suddenness always conquered me, beginning with hyperventilation, followed by indescribable suffocation. Think of quicksand. Then death.

I had never experienced a panic attack until I was 27. But believe me when I say, sadly I came to know this unwelcomed wickedness cursing me with *fear of the fear*. The invasion was so intense I felt as if I could literally jump out of my skin. The pounding of my heart caused my chest to hurt physically. This surge of energy, so powerful, left me with the strangely undeniable sensation that I could resurrect the dead. Maybe that's what I was trying to do!

As was the case with so many Americans, on September 11, 2001, fear shattered the beautiful, crystal blue Indian summer sky, the serenity of my patio, and my morning coffee as I witnessed the devastation and destruction of the World Trade Center. That day I experienced overwhelming sadness at the senseless loss of life. But in all honesty, it was the terror on the faces of those running for safety that haunted me. While they raced across those crumbling sidewalks of New York City, I ran with them through the daunting, dark, endless corridor that had become my life. On my patio, as I placed my cup of coffee on the wrought iron table, I wept and prayed for them – and for myself: *God save their souls*.

Those assailed by a panic attack face two choices: fight or flight. To protect myself from any threat, real or perceived, I would become like Athena, the Olympian goddess of wisdom, strategy and war. As Athena I am the protector of all, especially those with my DNA code: double X chromosome. No one could fully comprehend my wrath when I felt actually threatened, not the lingering anxiety of possible danger, but real, palpable menace, those times when anger overrode fear, and the Jenny Lynn spoiling for a fight got her wish. With this strength, I defied gravity as my soul shook and quaked, fueled by every disgusting memory of Room 939.

And so, still today at the slightest hint of transgression, I am a fearless warrior. My battle cry is a clarion warning: *Don't mess with me – or mine. And mine are not only my family and friends, but anyone I see victimized.*

Gradually, albeit intermittently, I regained some of my old fighting spirit. But, over time, I realized I had a much steeper mountain to climb. Fear wasn't the only enemy who had a stronghold in my soul. An even stronger, more insidious foe had taken residence in me that night in Room 939: an unforgiving spirit. To defeat this one, I would need help. I would need the Redeemer.

9

Turbulence

Statesboro, Georgia, was the perfect place for me to grow up. The peaceful congeniality, mild climate, and active social calendar of this Southern town matched my sunny personality. And attending a small school like Bulloch Academy enabled me to form friendships that enrich my life to this day. Being a people person, I have always felt comfortable in a variety of settings, including the corporate atmosphere at Lockheed and the frenetic one at the Georgia World Congress Center, but it's no surprise that I landed back in Statesboro after those forays into big city life. I was also blessed to discover a vocation that allowed me to enjoy those same qualities professionally. All my life, I have moved among friends, family, and colleagues with ease and felicity. So, naturally, going back to work would be a balm to my tortured soul. Restoring normality and routine would be the first step in my search for some semblance of sanity.

But the Jenny Lynn who returned to work at Willingway Hospital four days after the assault was a fragmented shell of her former self. Whereas simplicity and spontaneity – being fully present in every moment – had previously characterized my workdays, now hesitation, doubt, and fear paralyzed me. My every step was halting, my every thought clouded by uncertainty. I remember sitting at my desk that Monday, zombie-like, barely able to remember the real Jenny Lynn. It was as if I were sitting beside a stranger, someone vaguely familiar yet also somehow hauntingly alien. I stared from my window at the patients gathering outside, in of all places, the Sunshine Building. I watched them chatting, in various stages of repair, as they too took those first tentative steps along the path to wholeness. Witnessing those faces creased with pain and despair, I thought to myself, "You think you have problems?" In truth they did. But by God, so did I. The design of the hospital hallways added to my misery. A long hallway with rooms on each side dissects Unit Two, making it look eerily like a hotel corridor. Every day as I would make my way around the hospital, it served as a constant reminder of the attack. People suffering from PTSD wage a perpetual fight to rid their minds of recurring images of their trauma, but having to navigate a place so similar to the scene of the assault made that task practically impossible for me. I called it the passageway to hell; every day it triggered the onset of a panic attack. When I entered that building, the sizzling current of anxiety still coursing through my body surged into a full-blown crackling, chaotic turbo charge of terror and nausea. Imagine a shell-shocked war veteran having to walk each day through a field littered with potholes and ditches while some grinning fiend orchestrates a cacophony of explosions and screams. My life had become a litany of cruel irony.

There was, however, one saving grace. My Willingway colleagues were a stalwart cadre who never left my side. Expert at helping people rebuild their broken lives, they loved me unconditionally and let me know it every day through strong hugs, gentle words of encouragement, and often the best gift of all – simple, every day, routine behavior, as if my life were normal after all.

Sometimes, it seems the rippling side effects of tragedy never end. One of the saddest consequences of Room 939 was another involuntary response seared into my psyche. The evil in the man who attacked me had nothing to do with his race. It had erupted from someplace deep within his darkened soul, far beneath his skin. Beauty may be only skin deep, but ugliness like that reaches to the depths of a person's being. But I couldn't see that far. All I saw was a black face totally void of human sympathy.

Now, as I look back on my youth and early adulthood, I think that perhaps during those years, I extrapolated the synchronicity of my life to include the whole world. I knew that evil existed, of course; I wasn't that naïve. But darkness didn't – it couldn't – touch me. Then, after Room 939, I veered to the opposite extreme. I knew a good and holy God had created the universe and He controlled everything, yet, His goodness notwithstanding, this world was a very, very dangerous place. Not only did evil lurk everywhere, it had a special grudge against me. My war was not over; I had a treacherous, relentless enemy who sought to destroy me. And, unfortunately, the only physical manifestation of this ubiquitous malevolence had been a black man. Consequently, I became especially afraid of African-American males. That is an especially difficult admission for a Southern woman to make, given the South's racial history. But I hope my readers will understand these feelings resulted not from prejudice, but from pure, unadulterated fear. Moreover, while I acknowledge my region's checkered past, I firmly believe, in many ways, Southern blacks and whites are closer than in any other place in America, if not the entire world. We understand each other, and share much in common, particularly a love of God and family. None of that mattered, however, when I teetered on the edge of panic every time I encountered a black male.

Often, I have thought that had we lived in Montana with its microscopic African-American population, I would have felt less threatened as I envisioned peace and restoration while living among the majestic plains and mountains of that state. Had Mark known of the nightmare that would control our lives, he would have moved us there. But I would have found no peace by running away. I know that now.

Nevertheless, in his never-ceasing compassion and love for me, Mark did even better. He moved mountains to help me. Not until I reopened those wounds to write this book did I fully realize the many sacrifices he made for me during the tumultuous years following the assault and throughout our married life. In the early days, he gave up career advancement and totally reconfigured his life to care for me. He knew he had to be home before dark each day. If my assailant had been the physical manifestation of evil, Mark, my partner and sentinel, was an envoy from heaven. He gave up all hobbies to spend his every waking moment dedicated to his wife's not losing her mind. Mark became my shield against the daily horrors. He constantly reassured me he would hold me, even though the touch of his loving arms made me cringe. How that must have hurt him! What courage and love to make that sacrifice! So often during those dark and threatening nights, Mark held the lifeless form of his wife - weak and limp – when, without warning, the night of November 28, 1990, reached its icy, clammy hand into my home yet again.

When those inevitable attacks came, I became a wild woman, a raving lunatic. Mark would always make certain I saw him locking the doors, securing the windows, and closing the shades. Often, I asked him to check them again. Despite every effort to protect me, my PTSD continued to beat me down. A medley of frightful scenarios kept playing in my mind with two common motifs: I was always screaming and fighting for my life, and these disturbances always involved a dark figure. Sometimes he would rob me. In other variations, he kidnapped me at an airport and drove me around the terminal in a bus, a mobile version of that hotel hallway. Other nights the attack was in a parking garage. Often, more than one predator would stalk me. Indeed, my world was a very dangerous, treacherous place.

It was a maddening, tormented existence that left me ragged and exhausted. I felt relief from the fear and anxiety only when I was too spent to care, and, at least for a while, apathy became my default state of mind.

As time passed and I moved into my 30s and 40s, the complexity and frequency of the dreams subsided somewhat, but I still faced one persistent challenge. At night when Mark would come into our bedroom while I was sleeping, I would unknowingly try to escape from him. Again and again and again!

But he wasn't the predator. He was the love of my life.

This involuntary reaction went on and on, for weeks, months, years as my dreams and subconscious melded into a formidable force that took me down a rabbit hole and transformed what should have been my safest haven into a chamber of horrors. It was almost as if our bedroom door had a number etched into it – 939! And I would fight the most loving, precious person in my life as if he were the dark man sent to ravage me.

When I was finally awake enough to realize it was Mark, the aftermath was always the same. I would lie back down and take a deep breath as if it were my last. In the darkness, as sadness and despair continued its hold on me, I recalled my once-upon-a-time, carefree life and would cry myself to sleep.

During the day as I experienced some peace of mind, Mark and I discussed my night terrors. What could he do? What could I do? I had no power to stem the onslaught of torment that surged from my subconscious mind. I had yet to name my demon, and therefore had no power over him – yet. I remember one thoughtful and substantive conversation between Mark and me: it was about our wedding vows expressed in 1986, when we pledged our faithfulness, for better, for worse, for richer, for poorer, in sickness or in health, to love and to cherish 'till death do us part. We never fathomed the possibility that in one of these crazed moments over which I had no control, I could even go so far as murder. My God, murder, leaving Mark's blood on my hands!

Now, I remember those sad and sorry days of my life and thank God for granting Mark the wisdom and grace to accept the unspeakable might actually be possible. Some night, having gotten lost again in her parallel existence, convinced she was back in the grasp of her tormentor, that cold blade pushing her back into Room 939, his loving wife was capable of anything – even murder.

Quietly, he removed his gun from his bedside table.

Diary Entries | December 1990 – May 1992

Dec. 7, 1990 – *Still not sleeping well. Suffered panic attack. Stomach upset. Sweating profusely. On my way to work.*

Dec. 14, 1990 – *Never knew Christmas shopping could be so excruciating. Malls, public places make me nervous. Frightened by a 10-year-old African American boy walking toward me. How in God's name can I be scared of a little boy?*

Dec. 16, 1990 – *Frightened of public bathrooms. Is someone waiting for me in one of the stalls?*

January 13, 1991 – *At 1:30 in the morning made Mark get up and check all the doors and windows. Frightened someone was in the house.*

March 18, 1991 – *Another panic attack in the parking lot of the video store. Thought I was going to be robbed.*

May 3, 1991 – *9:00 p.m. Leaving to spend the night with Mama. Terrified my home will be burglarized.*

July 21, 1991 – *Another panic attack. Standing in the kitchen, thought I saw someone out the back door. Realized it was only reflection of the den television.*

September 18, 1991 – *Frightened while crossing the parking lot to attend the annual Chamber of Commerce dinner.*

October 31, 1991 – *I no longer enjoy Halloween. I can't tell who is behind the mask.*

January 3, 1992 – *Suffered major panic attack at*

automatic bank teller machine. Hands trembling, heart racing.

March 15, 1992 – *Nightmare about intruder. Feared someone was in our home.*

May 18, 1992 – *Another nightmare. In the hotel corridor with the black man. Woke up physically drenched and emotionally drained...again.*

10

My Faithful Father

It's Sunday morning, only 72 hours since the attack. I lie in bed listening to Mark's soft breathing as he sleeps, at least for him, a moment of calm amidst the storm that has wrecked our lives. He is exhausted. I am numb, a welcome state of mind, compared to the previous three days – and to what is to come. Ordinarily, we spend our Sunday mornings reading the dailies while enjoying coffee and one another's company.

Ordinarily – what an underappreciated word. I ache for the ordinary.

But on this Sabbath, as I lie there dazed and disoriented, I hear voices, not the frightening ones that will bring me such misery in the years to come, but the chatter of children as they bounce into a Sunday School room, the sweet voice of the dear woman telling them about her Savior, and the echoes of those good "ole timey" hymns heard in churches all around the South every Sunday morning about this time. As I struggle to recover the Jenny Lynn who went missing three days ago, images of the freshly-scrubbed little girl eager to hear more about Mrs. Beasley's friend awaken in me a yearning for something I misplaced many years ago, long before Room 939.

And then I hear another voice, a discordant note intruding on this brief moment of peace. The voice is my own.

"God have mercy on me! God save me!"

As the light and warmth of the morning sun bathe our bed, I feel His presence. A quiet voice answers, and I begin to listen, as the Shepherd takes my hand.

> *I am here, child. Come. We have far to go. The way will be steep at times, and rocky, and dark. But I will lead you, and I will never leave your side. Even when the mists cloud your vision and you cannot see me, I will be beside you. Always remember, I am here.*

I won't pretend my faith was completely restored that morning. If that were the case, the title of this book would be *Room 939: Fifteen Minutes of Horror, Three Days of Healing*. But, I did realize in those few minutes of peace the same God who heard me that night had never really left me. Those warm sunbeams confirmed what I had missed somehow – or had long forgotten. He is always with us. Jesus told his disciples they – and we – would have tribulation in this world, but that we should not be afraid because He had overcome the world. I should have treasured this beautiful truth in my heart. Perhaps I had at one time, but that little girl forgot her Sunday School lessons before she knew the Lord well enough to really trust Him.

My prodigal wandering began when I was promoted from Mrs. Beasley's class. I was eight. It all took place during Sunday School when our new teacher issued an apparently non-negotiable new policy: we would be required to pray out loud at the end of class. Though I was fond of the spotlight, I found myself painfully shy at the thought of praying in front of my class. That Bible study session, once fun and enjoyable in Mrs. Beasley's room, became an hour of high anxiety, so scary, in fact, that I stopped going to church – for the next 20 years! As a result, I became your "Easter Sunday Baptist" and finished my formative years basically un-churched.

And so, my journey back home began that first Sunday morning after the assault, and although I could not have articulated it so beautifully, somewhere deep inside my soul, amidst the howling fears that had taken residence there, a "still, small voice" said something else to me. In one way or another, Charles K. Robinson offers this beautiful benediction to all his wayward children:

> *You have fled as you now know-from my love,*
> *... but I love you nevertheless and not-the-less*
> *however far you flee. It is I who sustains your very*
> *power of fleeing, and I will never finally let you*
> *go. I accept you as you are ... I also know all the*
> *little tricks by which you try to hide the ugliness*
> *you have made of your life from yourself and others.*
> *But you are beautiful. You are beautiful more deeply*
> *within than you can see. You are beautiful because*
> *you yourself, in the unique person that only you*
> *are, reflect already something of the beauty of my*
> *holiness in a way which shall never end. You are*
> *beautiful also because I, and I alone, see the beauty*
> *you shall become. Through the transforming power*
> *of my love which is made perfect in weakness you*
> *shall become perfectly beautiful. You shall become*
> *perfectly beautiful in a uniquely irreplaceable way,*
> *which neither you nor I will work out alone, for we*
> *shall work it out together.*

Well, if He had the power, I sure had the weakness. With that I gently reached over, awakened Mark, and said quietly, "We're going to church."

As I stood in the shower, the conviction of His power was the only real thing I could feel. I said to myself, *Jenny Lynn, you called on Him in Room 939. It is time for you to allow Him back into your life and restore your relationship with Him.* I had taken my first step in learning how to become a faithful servant for the rest of my life.

Returning to church was a challenge. It felt as if I were coming home; only I didn't recognize any of my relatives. They spoke a foreign language. Bible passages, so familiar to me now, sounded unintelligible that morning. I had no context, and I began to understand the consequences of not having grown up in church. I felt as uncomfortable in that pew as I had when my childhood pastor delivered those stern sermons.

"Please turn to the book of Obadiah," said the preacher, and everyone around me turned skillfully through their well-worn Bibles to the assigned passage.

Obadiah, Obadiah. I don't think I've even heard of that one. Matthew, Mark, Luke, and John – why couldn't today's lesson be from one of those? I could find them. Maybe even one of the epistles. And Revelation. I know it's at the end. I could turn right to that one. But, Obadiah? Lord, have mercy on my soul!

Without the foundation of a church upbringing, I knew about Jesus, but I didn't know **Him**. Nor did I grasp the meaning of one of the most beautiful words in any language: *grace*. Yes, I had accomplished much in my young life. I had graduated college, married a good man, and embarked on a promising career in a field I loved. But none of that – and nothing I will ever do – could make me acceptable to God. Because Christ died for my sins, and for no other reason, my Father has imputed the Son's righteousness to me. When he looks at the ledger of my life, he doesn't see all the things Jenny Lynn has done and has left undone. He sees the spotless, debt-free account of Jesus Christ.

I know this gospel truth now, but that Sunday morning, the prodigal Jenny Lynn lacked the understanding to bring meaning to those promises found from Genesis to Revelation. I didn't even know the difference between the Old Testament and the New Testament. In short, I was biblically illiterate. Ignorance may be bliss, but, as I sat in that unfamiliar sanctuary, it was uncomfortably embarrassing. I did recall one verse, though, one that perhaps more than any other epitomizes the childlike faith I had lost for so long. From that moment, it became my banner of hope in those early years – *"For God so loved the world He gave His only begotten Son ..."* (John 3:16).

There was something else I needed to learn about God's grace, too. I had scrubbed my body clean that night in the hotel, but that man had touched places no soap and water ever could. I left Atlanta feeling permanently stained, tainted – damaged goods. I desperately needed to know that the Lamb's blood had long ago made that part of me eternally clean and that nothing and no one, not even my intruder, could touch me there. In his gospel, Mark recounts how the Pharisees criticized the disciples for eating without having washed their hands, therefore violating the ritual cleanliness laws. Jesus responded that nothing that goes into people from the outside makes them unclean. The same is true of anything that happens to us.

One does not learn these truths in a moment, however. That Sunday morning marked only the beginning of my healing, mentally and spiritually. Jenny Lynn had taken a fall and had been broken into many pieces. All the King's horses and all the King's men couldn't put Jenny Lynn back together again. But the King could. And He would, but He would do it in His time, teaching me lessons when I was ready to learn them. I knew God had allowed me to survive that horrible, heart wrenching night because He had a mission for me. He would heal me, and He would make me an instrument of His healing for others.

For a long time, I didn't know God's plans for me, for I had to learn to walk by faith and not by sight. And I had to learn patience.

Wait, Jenny Lynn, and My Word will lead you. Be patient. Be ready. Be sensitive to My Spirit as you hear My story from Genesis to Revelation. Hymns, prayers, and sermons will guide you, as will circumstances and conversations, friends and strangers. You will learn in times of quiet reflection and even when the noise of the world and of your fears will seem to crowd Me out of your life. For now, just take the next step and do the duty that lies nearest. That's all I ask you to do. That's all I will ever ask you to do.

Remarkably, His message soon began to crystallize – bit by bit.

Jenny Lynn, tell people how you called on me and how I answered you, how I still answer your pleas. Look into the faces around you. You are only one of many who hurt and who walk in fear. You will find them sitting by you in church and singing praises in Sunday School. They wait for you in the grocery aisle. They sit beside you during Friday night football games. They are everywhere, Jenny Lynn – the lost, those who know nothing about me. You have no time for pity, Jenny Lynn. Self-pity is of the devil. My world is hurting, and I will use you to ease that pain – if you obey. If you obey, all my power is at your disposal. But you will obey only if you have the faith that comes from knowing me.

I'd love to report I immediately became transformed into a mighty warrior, but truthfully, for the next decade, my life became a tug of war between God's holy promises and Satan's destructive weapons of panic and fear. Sunlight had bathed our bedroom with peace that morning, but the sun had set that evening, and darkness once again overwhelmed me, inside and out. So, for many years, my home remained a place where I merely existed. I began to learn those hymns of praise that sounded so strangely familiar, yet painfully alien that morning, and I soon began to know my way around Scripture pretty well, but all too often the attacker's guttural voice snuffed out the light that had begun to flicker in my soul. During those dark times of doubt, I tried with all my might to turn to Him in prayer with the same sense of need as I had in 939 or in the quiet peace of that Sunday morning in our bedroom. Night after night, I wept for relief, for strength to move totally onto God's side. But honestly, for too long, I allowed Satan to be the victor, as panic and fear controlled me. God had made me a promise:

"Never will I leave you; never will I forsake you" (Hebrews 13:5).

He kept that promise, of course. He had never left me, even in 939, but so often in the years to come, I would strain to hear His "still small voice" amidst the whirlwind that would rage about me.

11

Happy Faces

We've all heard some version of the "nurture vs. nature" debate. Are we products of our heredity – nature – or of our circumstances – nurture (or in some cases the lack thereof)? Surely who we are results from a combination of influences. Some of us seem "hardwired" with an abundance of energy and optimism, while others can hardly get off the couch and never see the upside of any situation. Some prefer chocolate; others like vanilla. Some poor souls don't like ice cream at all! As Louis Armstrong once sang, "You like tomato; I like tomahto ..." But when it comes to family, we can't "call the whole thing off."

It's like they say: we can choose our friends, but we can't choose our family. And I believe they influence us the most, producing personalities "geometrically" shaped by the atmosphere in our homes. Some clans, for example, are just naturally *square* – all white bread, vanilla ice cream, and sugar cookies, about as electrifying as a kerosene lamp. They're perfectly good people, mind you; it's just that it's nice to have a little caramel syrup on your ice cream and a few sprinkles on your cookies every now and then, maybe even a loaf of sourdough. Walk into their museum – uh, home – greet them with a jovial "Hey everybody! How are ya?" and they respond "Fair. Not bad." I never could understand "not bad." How can you be "not bad?" How about "good," "excellent," "couldn't be better!" There are, of course, times when it's impossible to put on a happy face. I had to learn that lesson the hard way, but, all things being equal, I've always believed in making the best of every situation.

Then there is the true "family circle" clan whose homes teem with activity. They're the ones where all the teenagers congregate after school and on weekends. Their doors are perpetually open and welcoming. Dinner tables buzz with lively conversation and genuine camaraderie. The warmth in these houses attracts fun and fellowship like a campfire on an autumn night. These are the Italians and the Greeks and others who live large. They kiss right smack on the mouth, hug at every opportunity, and serve wine with every meal.

My family? Well, we were a *triangle*. Mother was the base; Janna and I the two identical sides. Daddy's reserved nature complemented the energy of the three women of the house, a judge, a future lawyer, and, well, me. With Mama's being the dominant presence in our home, he found reticence the better part of valor.

Janna and I enjoyed a consistent, loving relationship with Mama, who demonstrated no favoritism, but rather treasured us both. Thus, the blessings of our triangular connection enabled our mother-daughter-daughter relationship to grow evenly and substantially as Janna and I matured into young women.

But while that tightly-knit symmetry has blessed us immeasurably, it can have its downside. When one of us is hurting, the other two know it. When you're so connected to someone, it's practically impossible to hide your pain from her. So, I knew that opening up to Mama about my nightmares meant she would likely tell Janna to enlist her support. Likewise, if I confided in Janna, she would speak to Mother for the same reason. I guess it takes two sides of a triangle to hold up the third one. I thank God every day for Mark, Mama, and Janna to lean on, but I tried many times to put on that old Jenny Lynn face just to lighten their burden, if only for a while.

And so, as time passed and my emotional wounds remained open and raw, I did all I could to spare them my pain. As powerless as I felt at times against the forces that oppressed me, I did my best to bear the brunt of the anxiety and panic that often engulfed me. If words or hugs or shared anger or laughter could have healed me, I would soon have been the old Jenny Lynn, for they showered me with all these remedies and more. But they knew that I hurt in a place they couldn't see and couldn't touch.

At least for a while, the triangle had to be broken apart, and I had to make a long, perilous journey without them. Writing to the church at Ephesus, the Apostle Paul warned those new believers they faced a different kind of enemy. *"For our struggle is not against flesh and blood,"* he told them, *"but against the rulers, against the authorities, against the powers of this dark world and against the spiritual forces of evil in the heavenly realms"* (Ephesians 6:12). I had been thrust into battle against those terrifying, invisible foes, and I had escaped with my life, but the fight had just begun. The Lord would provide me with all the weapons I would need to prevail, but it would be a long time before I knew how to put on that full armor. In the meantime, my family would gladly have stood in the gap for me, but I was determined that if the enemy won, I would be his only trophy.

I could see the stress and concern, as a high tide of tears would appear in Janna's eyes as if each onslaught of my fear and anxiety were a new moon pulling her into my darkness. I could read her face like my own.

How could this have ever happened to Jenny Lynn? Look at her! Where is my joyful, exuberant sister? Whose eyes are those? Not Jenny Lynn's, not the girl whose smile welcomed everyone she met into her heart. Does that monster have any idea what treasure he stole from her – from all of us?

At night, at home alone, Mother, too, wept for her daughter. Though I bound my wounds as tightly as I could, a child cannot hide her pain from her mother. My agony became hers and Janna's as if transmitted via an invisible network. That's what it was, really. This endearing duet I loved so deeply was dying right alongside me, a fact that only added to my torment.

I did my best to maintain control when around them. I muted the volume so they couldn't hear the screams that sounded so clearly in my head. Attempting to bring some normalcy – longing for the beautiful ordinary, I'd try to steer our conversations to anything other than my situation. And, of course, they would do their best to play along. But we all knew better.

Janna, with her perception inherited from our mother, the Superior Court Judge, remained tuned into to my state of mind. A personal injury attorney, Janna possessed the keen insight and logical mind that made her a fearless and able courtroom fighter as she defended those suffering both physically and mentally. Like all good lawyers, she is adept at reading people, but she has always been particularly expert at deciphering the Jenny Lynn code. Years of late-night talks about boys and school, hopes and dreams, secrets and fears made us a simpatico pair of sisters. In some ways, Janna has always known me better than anybody.

Although I never completely shut her or Mama out, I did erect a hard, protective shell that kept them at an unnatural, awkward distance. So, for two decades, Janna, especially, chipped away at that fortress. Gentle at times. Firm at times. But constant: "Jenny Lynn, are you doing okay? Is there anything still bothering you? Are you still having those thoughts?" I would simply say, "I'm fine Janna. It's not bothering me as much anymore." That was that – end of story. She knew I was lying, of course, just as I knew she was when she'd reply, "Okay, I was just checking." My sister, always the better athlete, didn't stand a chance in this test of endurance. After all, I had seen combat. She hadn't. So, we'd drop the subject and go on pretending the elephant wasn't there – and ache silently for the ordinary.

It wasn't a victory I claimed proudly. As teenage athletes, Janna and I always wore down any opponent unlucky enough to compete against us. But this was a quest I had to make without her – at least for a season, a long season. As time wore on and I began to grasp the power of the Word, I learned to use the weapons Christ forged for us all in the fires of Gethsemane and Calvary. If I had known then the truths I know now, I would have enlisted Janna to fight with me.

Where two or more are gathered together in My name ...

Until I learned the power of prayer, though, I had no idea if I would survive this unsuspected war. In the meantime, I resolved to make sure of one thing: neither my sister nor my mother would be casualties of Room 939.

12

Tug of War

A wise man once told me that the moment my ravaged body slid down the door inside that hotel room, I became a survivor. He was right, of course. I had escaped with my life – my physical life at least. But, the Jenny Lynn who returned to Statesboro with her mother was not the same optimistic dynamo who had left for Atlanta only a few days earlier. I and everyone who loved me had to wonder if we would find that happy young woman with the boundless future ever again. Had she been destroyed in Room 939? Had she retreated to some dark place deep inside herself, a haven where evil could not hurt her again? Like many suffering from PTSD, I became detached from others, unable to summon my old enthusiasm and optimism. I loved Mark and the rest of my family as much as before, but I lacked the energy to show them. Whereas I had always been spontaneous and uninhibited, especially around those close to me, now my every gesture seemed stiff and forced.

But I had not lost all my passion. Rather, I channeled much of it into a poisoned obsession. I became a bitter, angry woman, fixated on a question that haunts every one of us at some point in our lives: the problem of evil. *Why do bad things happen to good people?*

Hadn't I been a good little girl growing up? Hadn't I done all the right things? Obeyed all the rules? I had finished school, married a good man, and begun a promising career. I was one of the good guys. Right?

My record was not spotless, of course. Jenny Lynn had been naughty on occasion, maybe on a few occasions. I never took a guilt trip as a child, but I did have a conscience to prick me when I did wrong. Like most children, especially those forced to endure the threats of fire and brimstone that rain down from some pulpits, I'm sure I thought of God as a cosmic judge, who, if I were to stand before Him, would look upon me with disappointment and disapproval as he perused my two childhood accounts of misbehavior.

The first happened when I was six years old. Somehow, during a routine shopping trip with Mom to the Piggly Wiggly, a roll of Zotz Fizz Power Candy made its way out of the store unbeknownst to my mother – and the cashier. Oh, how I savored those light pink discs as they fizzed luxuriously in my mouth, but the froth, fulfillment and the yum were short lived. As Mama slid into the front seat for our drive home, my "telltale heart" burst open, and I admitted my crime. My confession lifted my burden, and the truth had set me free! Sort of.

Judge Martin pronounced her sentence immediately and marched me right back inside to repay my debt to society. I was to apologize to the store manager and in a voice loud and clear. With cheeks burning, I confessed for the second time as the shoppers waiting in the check-out lines shook their heads, and a refrain of "tsk tsks, for shame, for shame" rained down upon me. At least that's what I heard. Then, I did the "perp walk" to a front door that seemed a mile away, a scarlet "T" for thief etched clearly on my forehead.

While I'm at it, I guess I should come completely clean and admit to frequently dropping by my neighbor's garage to sample Lucky's Dry Dog Food, an affinity for which I can't really account. That tasty concoction must have supplied some essential nutrient missing from my regular diet. At any rate, I suffered no ill effects from my canine snacking, although I did have an occasional, barely resistible urge to chase a passing car. Now that I think about it, maybe that's why I enjoyed following the "Skeeter Man" so much. I never peed on any bushes or fire hydrants, though. I promise.

We can all recall similar escapades from our childhoods, most of which we remember as fairly harmless, at least a little amusing, and often embarrassing. But incidents like these provide an important clue to the mystery of evil.

Sin has become a taboo subject in postmodern America. It's definitely not a topic for "polite company," and even when Godly pastors preach about it, we worry they will scare off the "seekers," those who come to church looking for something to fill the void in their lives. The fact is what they are seeking is Truth, and that's what they should hear. I'm so grateful that my pastor Dr. John Waters refuses to be intimidated by the derisive voices of those who say our theology smacks of judgment and self-righteousness. To the "enlightened," ours is an outdated, superstitious creed. Ask most any group whether they think children are born innocent only to be corrupted (some anyway) by society or if they believe that somehow the old Christian doctrine of original sin is true. Most, even many of the "churched," will agree with the first proposition.

To them, I would pose these questions: Why is it that little Jenny Lynn took that candy? Why do children tell white lies? Why is it that children are so often cruel to one another? The simple truth is that we don't have to teach kids to behave badly; instead, we have to teach them right from wrong. All of us arrive in this life self-centered and intent on getting our way.

But there is another half to the equation. Jenny Lynn took the candy, but she also knew in her heart that she had done wrong. The Apostle Paul had long "put away childish things" when he wrote his letter to the Roman church, but in it he spoke of a confounding inner struggle we all face, even as children:

"For I do not do the good I want to do, but the evil I do not want to do – this I keep on doing" (Romans 7:19).

And so, no matter how hard we try to deny them, we cannot escape two indisputable truths: There is a moral law – and thus a moral Law-Giver – and, in one way or another, we just keep on breaking it. That's why Jenny Lynn took the candy, and that's why she confessed to her mother only a few minutes later.

But, as I lay in a shattered heap on that hotel room floor, the imprint of a knife blade still fresh on my neck, I cared nothing for theological speculations. They would have provided me no comfort that night and wouldn't have begun to answer the question that formed on my lips as soon as that coward ran away:

Why me Lord? What could I possibly have done to deserve this?

I knew the answer already. Nothing! No one deserves to suffer like that at the hands of another human being, and God most certainly does not mete out justice this way. The devastation in Room 939 did not take place to balance some cosmic accounts ledger. So, I was left asking, sometimes, screaming *"Why?"*

I still haven't found the answer. As I've gotten to know

the Lord better, I don't ask it as much. One day, maybe not until I stand in His presence, I'll hear God's reply. Perhaps I'll receive an even greater grace. Perhaps the question will no longer matter.

I must admit, though, that during those years of anger and frustration, suffering and searching, I thought of so many others who deserved His wrath more than I. At least I thought so. I made mental lists, penciled in names, and recorded their bad deeds. I became the third attorney in my family. Only I was a prosecutor, building a case against all those truly deserving of God's punishment – and against God himself. Surely, He had erred. Or maybe he was capricious, handing out punishment willy nilly, without regard for justice. Or worse, maybe he had forgotten me – or had been powerless to stop the evil that had assaulted me. That was the most chilling thought of all. Regardless, Room 939 should never have happened. I tried to settle for a lie I never came close to actually believing. "Well, God, you just made a mistake and I have to live with it."

But, Jenny Lynn, He is perfect! God never makes mistakes.

I longed to be able to say as had Job near the end of that enigmatic story, "*I know that you can do all things; no purpose of yours can be thwarted ... Surely I spoke of things I did not understand, things too wonderful for me to know*" (Job 42: 2-3).

But, Jenny Lynn did not have the proverbial patience of Job. For a very long time, I doubted God's perfection, His power, and most of all, His love for me. From a deep pit of despair, I continued to wonder, "Was I not worthy of His power to save me?" With all my might, I struggled to regain control of my destiny and muster at least a trace of faith. I had yet to learn, however, that faith, like forgiveness, does not result from human effort. They are the free gifts of grace, bought and paid for by a Savior's blood. But we have to come – or be brought – to a place where we can accept those treasures.

Hatred and an unforgiving spirit, no matter how humanly justifiable, give Satan legal right to harden our hearts as he stokes the fires of righteous indignation and resentment – and fear, always the fear. He was in the driver's seat, and we hurtled toward a cliff – and the final crash that would kill my spirit once and for all. At times, I think I probably wished for that collision.

As months and years passed, the endless struggle continued, at times erupting into a flaming conflagration, at others settling into gritty, grinding war of psychological and spiritual attrition. Now and then, for no obvious reason, the battlefield would fall silent, and Satan would leave me for a season. During those brief ceasefires, I was in control. Taking a long shower, preparing a leisurely breakfast for Mark and me, waving to him as he left for work, spending an afternoon shopping with friends – for a precious while, I could once again enjoy these simple pleasures. The extraordinary ordinary!

It was during those respites that I reclaimed a glimpse of my old self. And oh... how I loved her - a captivating, animated storyteller – an adventurer seeking discovery and finding opportunity in every challenge. Had I been the committed Christian I am now, I would have gone to Romans 8:38-39 to find the spiritual conviction I needed. With Satan's lies silenced, I could have embraced this eternal truth: *"For I am convinced that neither death nor life, nor angels nor demon ... nor anything else in all creation will be able to separate us from the love of God ..."*

But Satan always renewed his attacks, and like a desert

mirage, the old Jenny Lynn faded away once more. It was as if I had awakened from a beautiful dream, as though my momentary joy had been merely a tantalizing vision to remind me of what I had lost. The questions returned, too, and the bitterness.

Why didn't God take care of business once and for all? Why won't He fight for me and give me my life back? Is this hell after all? Is there even such a thing as peace? **God, where are you?**

Still no answer. Years would pass with no release. I floundered in a sea of despondency and came perilously close to coming ashore at the one place Satan most desired – the land of hopeless, irretrievable despair, the state of mind completely void of faith. Smothered beneath a blanket of lies, I remained ignorant of another jewel of truth that could have given me great comfort, one that I hope my readers will take from my story and hold tightly when they feel powerless against Satan's attacks. Twice in the life of our Lord, His enemy summoned every evil power at his disposal to attack Him. The first was in the wilderness at the beginning of Christ's three-year ministry. The second was in the Garden of Gethsemane. The first Adam had succumbed to Satan's wiles in another garden. Had Jesus done the same, all would indeed be lost forever. The lesson, dear reader, is this: The devil does not waste his time attacking those who pose him no threat. If he is after you, rest assured that God has a mighty plan for you. God did not ordain the horror of Room 939, but "we know that in all things," even our darkest horrors, "*God works for the good of those who love him, who have been called according to his purpose*" (Romans 8:28). Your life *does* have meaning. God *will* bless you. He *will* use you.

I know that now, but in the meantime, until she could grasp the sword of truth, Jenny Lynn had to find a way to keep fighting – and survive.

13

The Girls

⸻◦◦◦⸺

"Therefore shall a man leave his father and his mother, and shall cleave unto his wife: and they shall be one flesh." Genesis 2:24

From the beginning, God ordained marriage as the bedrock of human civilization. It was the flesh and blood manifestation of the divine Trinity, that eternal dance of selfless love and joy. In one sense, marriage reflects the Trinity because it is a circle of love comprised of three distinct human personalities, not just two. God said, and Jesus later affirmed, the husband and wife "shall be one flesh." As God intended marriage, man and woman bring their unique selves to this holy union, yet retain their distinct identities. But just as great artists match colors so that each enhances the beauty of the other, a marriage with Christ at its center joins a man and a woman so complementarily that their union itself has a personality all its own. There is the husband, there is the wife, and there is the couple; the two together producing a unique third comprised of "one flesh."

In another sense, of course, the third is God Himself, and men and women who love God first and most love one another all the more. As C.S. Lewis once wrote, "You can't get second things by putting them first; you can get second things only by putting first things first." In other words, put God first, and He will bless all your "second things," especially your marriage. I am, of course, describing the ideal here. In this fallen world, we bring very imperfect selves to even the best of marriages. So, we work and we work, and bit by bit, we learn to love after God's design.

Then, there are children, that most precious gift. Though many blessed marriages remain childless, most couples want to expand their circle of love to include children, and certainly most young girls dream of becoming moms. I suspect that boys, too, have a natural yearning for fatherhood. Nothing softens the heart of a man like holding his newborn child. Yes, we often make a mess of it, but family is one of God's greatest blessings. Naturally, then, the enemy seeks to destroy it.

He certainly did his best to ruin my marriage to Mark. Not long after I returned from Atlanta, a chilling realization stung me, something that had lingered somewhere in my mind in the days following the assault but that I had struggled to avoid facing. Then, suddenly, it hit me with stunning clarity. The obscenity of Room 939 would extend to our marriage bed! Had the invasion torn apart what God had joined together on our wedding day? The awful rippling effects of sexual trauma violate the lives of its victims in ever widening circles. It nearly destroyed me; it devastated Mark, who would have given anything to get his hands on my assailant, and it very nearly ruined our chances of ever again sharing our love in the most beautiful and intimate way. The thought that Mark and I might not be able to redeem what the man had taken from us terrified me. Even now, I shudder to think that our two beautiful daughters might never have been born, that today my marriage might be a distant memory, a victim of Room 939.

Every little girl wants her own baby doll, to care for, to protect and to love unconditionally. Mine was Chatty Cathy.

She was a gift from Santa when I was six. From the moment I laid eyes on my blue-eyed, blond haired baby, I knew if I really cared for and loved Chatty Cathy the way good mamas do, one day I would get to be a real mom. As I drew back the string, its release offered sweet phrases: "Please brush my hair," "Take me with you" and "May I have a cookie?" Even at the age of six I felt those motherly instincts.

My most favorite of her "coos" was a reassuring, "I love you." It seems just a second ago I was looking into Chatty Cathy's eyes dreaming of the day I would have girls of my own.

My late 20s seemed the perfect time for Mark and me to begin working on our dream of starting a family. We were reasonably established professionally and very happy domestically. The next stage in our adventure was obvious – until Room 939.

Evil is completely unoriginal. It cannot create; it can only destroy the beautiful. Void of anything lovely, it seethes with envy and seeks to pervert what it cannot have. And so, another "third" became part of our marriage. A malignant presence lingered about our bedroom, turning our every attempt at intimacy into heartbreak. I could not allow myself to be held and loved by this man who had never left my side. It seemed that what God had joined together had indeed been torn asunder and our dream of having children would be yet another casualty of that night in Atlanta.

I remember confiding in Dr. Al Palmer, my Ob-Gyn and close friend, during a routine check-up. "How can I possibly conceive when the truth of the matter is, intimacy is out of the question?" "Jenny Lynn," he responded, "The healing of your mind must take place first." I will always remember Dr. Palmer's warmth, compassion, and understanding. Godly men and women who submit to His will become Jesus' literal hands and feet. Dr. Palmer was one of many whom God used to speak to me, and that day, his words resonated as I walked to the car and confirmed what I already knew in my heart. I had to find my way back to my husband's arms.

I continued praying God would restore our marriage bed and rekindle our dreams of bringing new life into the world. Although my view of that world had been poisoned, I still believed in family. I knew Mark and I could provide a safe and loving home. I resolved to see to it that our children, should God bless us with them, would relish life with the optimism and eager anticipation that had been stolen from me. Now, as I look back on those prayers, I realize they were evidence of a growing faith I wasn't aware of at the time. If I had truly believed all hope was lost and I could not trust God, starting a family would have been out of the question. Someone once said our sons and daughters are God's way of saying the world should continue. I believe my thoughts about motherhood were partly His telling me that I must continue, too:

Jenny Lynn, you must not lose hope. Life is still worth it. You will see.

Before I left his office, Dr. Palmer had given me one last bit of advice. "Jenny Lynn, it might not be a bad idea to get out of town. Take a trip. Go somewhere. You never know what might happen."

Thinking maybe my physician and friend was on to something, I planned an August, 1991, vacation to Montego Bay with our friends Valerie and Glen. It was not an easy trip, and romance did not await me in Jamaica. The very idea of staying in a hotel room again terrified me, with safety my paramount concern. Even with

Mark by my side, I jumped at every noise, and my eyes darted about the airport terminal, an arcade of sudden movements. Rest and relaxation still eluded me in this exotic place where, unfortunately, the Jamaican men all reminded me of my attacker. Even the Caribbean's tropical beauty did little to chase away the anxiety, and the robust Jamaican Blue Mountain coffee and native food kept my stomach in somersaults. My romantic getaway was hell. But while I found no peace and tranquility in paradise, I did encounter another of life's little ironies, this one serendipitous.

During the last day of vacation as Valerie and I rode horses across the trails of Jamaica, I felt a sudden pang of nausea.

Well, of course, Jenny Lynn. No vacation from hell is complete without a good old-fashioned stomach virus. Might as well make room for more misery.

And misery it was! I retched throughout that night and into the morning we were to leave. I was barely able to hang on to Mark as we trekked through the airport. Then, while Glen bought souvenirs with the remnants of his Jamaican money, I made it to the bathroom one more time before we departed.

The morning after we arrived home found a dehydrated and exhausted Jenny Lynn at her doctor's office cramped and complaining of "Montezuma's revenge." Fifteen minutes later, with blood work results in hand, the nurse explained in simple terms, the cause and name of the "virus." She said, "Honey, you're pregnant."

God, in his infinite mercy, had affirmed me once again.

Jenny Lynn, blessed be the tie that binds your heart with mine. We are not done yet, you and I.

Today, I can look back at those days of uncertainty, doubt, and confusion with clarity unavailable to one in the midst of a storm. I didn't know it then, but even in the darkest of times, the Lord was putting the mosaic of my life back together piece by piece, those tiles bound together by the beautiful promise made to all who call on Him:

"For I know the plans I have for you ... plans to prosper you and not to harm you, plans to give you hope and a future" (Jeremiah 29:11).

And so, my womb became a cradle of birth and rebirth as faith, hope – and Morgan Elizabeth Anderson – grew a little larger and a little stronger every day.

When I looked into our baby girl's angelic face, I could only marvel at God's grace. During the two years following Room 939, when I had recoiled at the thought of marital love and when it looked as if our marriage would indeed be ripped apart, Mark and I had shared only one moment of intimacy. Instead of a sanctuary, our bedroom had become a stark reminder of conjugal joy we had lost. It was not lost forever, of course. It lay hidden behind a cloud of lies, but the demons of deceit could not thwart God's plans, not even in the darkest of times.

And so, we all lived happily ever after. Motherhood restored Jenny Lynn to her old self, her fears disappeared, and all was right again in her universe.

Uh, no, not exactly.

Blessed by the presence of my first born, I wanted more than anything for those early days with Morgan to be filled with joy and unconditional love. But PTSD does not surrender so easily. My fight with it wore on, and in many ways I was a weakened warrior. As it is, new mothers face perhaps the greatest "ordinary" challenge of their lives. They've just spent nine months on a hormone-induced emotional roller coaster inside a body they hardly recognize, followed by the throes of labor and birth. Then, they come home exhausted, hormones still raging, to the joys of 3 a.m. feedings, dirty diapers, and haunting doubts. I faced all that with a hundred pound millstone of PTSD around my neck. I loved being a mother, but still the enemy stole away what should have been many precious moments with my daughter – for weeks, then months, then years.

As I rocked Morgan in the wee hours of the morning, every creaking board whispered, "I'm going to get you again." Tree branches blowing in the rustling breeze transmogrified into dark figures brandishing knife blades and lunging at me. Shapes, barely discernible in the darkness, morphed into threatening ogres. Unable to tune out the maddening chorus, I would carry her back to the crib, heave a weary sigh, and collapse into bed, my body drenched. The hope and faith that had taken on new life in my womb shriveled. Not even my beautiful daughter's eyes could lift the blanket of despair that engulfed me once again.

Only now the fear was worse. Since I had "discovered" how dangerous the world really was, I became even more afraid for my defenseless infant. At least I could fight back, but she lay helpless against the ubiquitous threats I saw coming at us. It was inevitable, then, that from the beginning, I would be an overprotective mother. A parade of sordid scenarios streamed through my tortured mind, revealing the worst possible outcome to any situation. While at work one day, I learned to my horror that our nanny had allowed two strangers to tour our home, which we had put on the market. If most people begin their day with their anxiety meters registering a three or four on a scale of ten, with ten being raging panic, PTSD sufferers greet most every morning with the needle already in the red zone, seven or eight at least, and ready to explode at the slightest hint of "emergency." So when I heard about those visitors, my mind immediately flashed to images of a somber newscaster reporting on the Anderson kidnapping that had taken place in Statesboro. By the time I had coaxed the needle back to a manageable eight, the nanny was looking for new employment.

My travails continued as I struggled to gain some grip on reality, however tenuous. For instance, when Morgan was four months old, I noticed a small, scaly, red patch on her face. Swoosh! The "Angst O Meter" is at ten again. A frantic search through *Dr. Spock's Baby and Child Care* brought no reassuring answers, so, exhausted and frustrated, I made an appointment with a dermatologist who took one look at Morgan's face and provided me his diagnosis: atopic dermatitis. Heart pounding, I asked, "What is that?" "Jenny Lynn, it's a common and chronic skin disease that affects a lot of people. It's called eczema." I became completely derailed.

Common? Okay. Chronic? No! Not this time! No more chronic! My child will not be a prisoner of chronic anything! I may not be able to fix myself, but I'm going to fix this. I will find the answer.

PTSD had taken hold of my mind. Truth be known, there is no cure for eczema. But, at least this rash was a tangible enemy. I knew I would find the answer, so I tackled this new challenge with the same intensity I had poured into researching the PTSD that fueled this frenzied response in the first place. Finally, however, I had to resign myself to the fact that eczema could be controlled, but not cured.

Of course, having become thoroughly conditioned to immediately extrapolate to the worse possible outcome, my mind filled with images of a sad, lonely little girl unable to play tennis, cheerlead, wade in the surf, go away to camps – or enjoy a harmless hayride with a nice Southern boy.

Fortunately, though, the poisonous pessimism that had backed me into a corner did not affect my DNA. Throughout her duel with eczema, Morgan proved more than able to meet the challenge, having inherited the toughness and cheerful optimism of her mother and father. With the heart of a lion, she displayed courage and determination, meeting every challenge childhood and adolescence threw at her, including the eczema that plagued her into her teens. She did, thank you very much, excel in sports, winning the number one doubles match at the State High School Tennis Tourney during her senior year. As she received her trophy, I thought I saw a tiny glint of the old Jenny Lynn in those victorious eyes.

By that time, she had a little sister to share her triumph. When Morgan was three, God blessed us with a healthy, blue-eyed, happy-go-lucky baby girl, Allison Faye. Because of her joyful nature, she earned nicknames like "Smiley" and "Little Miss Sunshine" throughout preschool. And let me say right here and now all children are designed and delivered by God. And on each occasion He knows what He is doing. He truly did in this case understand my spiritual and maternal needs. With that, Allison would light up each of my mornings, where from her crib she would greet me with arms outreached to love me unconditionally. She was my angel with that happy face. When I held her, an undeniable sense of hope filled me. With my still being haunted by the darkness, this child broke through it all and brought joy to my aching heart and soul. As I said, God knows what He is doing.

I truly owe much of my healing to her. From the crib to this day, Allison has been a steady beam of sunshine. My dear friend Dawn Oliver delights in telling the story of Allison and Mark enjoying an afternoon at Chick-Fil-A. When they got up to leave, Allison stopped at every table to personally deliver a hearty goodbye to the guests. Our toddler already knew how to work the crowd.

And so, two bright rays of God's love had begun to slowly chase the shadows from the Anderson household. God's amazing grace had kept Mark and me together, and we had managed to have the family we had dreamed of. As I look at early photographs of my girls and me, I can see the old Jenny Lynn coming slowly into focus, like a picture downloading in the beginning days of the Internet, her features more clearly defined frame by frame. I see genuine, unabashed joy, glimpses of my true self.

Sporadically, but more frequently as those years wore on, I could look into the evening sky as the heavens declared the glory of God – light instead of darkness. Not every bump in the night would send me spiraling into panic mode. The anxiety meter sometimes even dipped below seven or eight.

What God had joined together, the forces of man and hell had not torn asunder.

14

My BFF
(Best Friend Forever)

"Where two or three are gathered together in My name, there am I in the midst of them." Matthew 18:20

It's amazing what God can do when a group of strangers comes together to study His Word. Many might think it uncomfortable to meet with women you don't know well to explore passages of Scripture. But that is exactly what I did when I walked into the Statesboro United First Methodist Church in August, 1997. I didn't know a soul in the room except Lee Cheshire, the group leader. Although I had been faithfully attending Church and Sunday School for seven years, I still couldn't find my way to the book of Isaiah on the first day of this women's Bible study. By this time, however, I had grown quite comfortable in God's house, so, although a bit uneasy, I didn't feel quite the embarrassment as on that Sunday morning I had first come "home." (By the way, something I learned years later, just eyeball your Bible and open it to the dead center of the book and chances are you'll land in the chapter of Isaiah). It should come as no surprise that our initial gathering didn't seem awkward. After all, we were family, members of the body of Christ, and He has promised to be in our midst any time we gather in His name.

Sitting there with this eclectic group of women, unable to find Isaiah, I had a Jenny Lynn "duh" moment.

It dawned on me that finding my way around the Bible wasn't nearly as important as letting go of the pride that made me feel uncomfortable in the first place. *So what if I couldn't find it? Who was going to judge me? God? He wanted me to find Him.* Remembering my discovery, I realize how particularly relevant one of the beatitudes was to me at that stage in my spiritual growth.

"Blessed are the meek, for they shall inherit the earth" (Matthew 5:5).

It's another of the Lord's stumbling block statements.

"Okay, so to be blessed, I have to become a mousy little pushover? The wimps and the milquetoasts are going to end up with all the good stuff?"

Wrong. The word meek comes from the Greek word praus, which means "gentle strength." It also means humble, another unattractive word in our culture. But, to be humble is to be teachable. The humble person says, "I don't know everything. In fact, there is an awful lot I don't know, but you know what? That's okay because I'm ready to learn." Meekness is one of the building blocks of wisdom.

That's why I was there, to learn, and so were the rest of our circle. I decided to purchase a bookmark guide that presented the Bible in chronological order. The next week I confessed to the group that having never been a biblical scholar, I was a bit nervous about this spiritual step I was about to take. "In fact," I said. "Although I am an educated woman, I feel downright stupid when it comes to the Scriptures." I went on to add how much I wanted to learn God's Word, and would be using my bookmark to help me find my way.

Blushing as I admitted my ignorance, I expected an

awkward silence. Instead, I got the surprise of my life when the lady sitting beside me turned and asked, "Do you have an extra one with you? I can't find my way around the Bible either." Suddenly, many were declaring their struggles in locating His Word. "Why, I'm not alone at all," I thought. It was a critical breakthrough for me. God had said, "Jenny Lynn, *Ask and it will be given to you; seek and you will find; knock and the door will be opened to you*" (Matthew 7:7).

From then on, I felt the power of the Holy Spirit, along with the love and support of my sisters in Christ. Those quiet meetings were mountaintop experiences for all of us, but we don't live on the acme atmosphere. We dwell in the demon-infested valley where trusting God is so much more difficult, especially when we pray with a heavy burden on our hearts and our prayers seem to go unanswered. Didn't Matthew 7:7 apply at all times in every situation? Even the most devout, committed Christians endure seasons when this promise rings hollow or, perhaps more likely, a devil's demonic presence convinces them they must be guilty of some hidden, unconfessed sin. On my walk, I encountered many such steep, rocky places where dust and wind pounded me, and hunger and thirst tortured me, bringing me to the point of giving up.

Each night, I pleaded with God to take away my pain and restore my soul. Having established a new relationship with Him, and believing He was my new BFF (Best Friend Forever), I knew God would be my fix-it fellow and miracle worker. Folks, let me just stop right here and tell you something really important about the so called Man upstairs. He is not the Wizard of Oz. But I wanted Him to be. I knew if He would allow me to click those ruby red slippers three times, I could return home where I would awaken from my nightmare surrounded by loved ones joyously relieved to have Jenny Lynn back.

Life would be perfect if we all had that magical "easy" button from Staples. I love those commercials! They promise an ease to life's frustrating problems. One touch of that bright, beckoning sphere and our troubles vanish.

I wanted God to be my easy button. But be assured there is no chapter in God's life-giving Book entitled "Simple." Simple *does not exist*. Therefore I remained chained to the dark man in the dark hall with the knife at my neck.

So, even with God by my side, the tempest still raged. At times, I felt maybe God was the Wizard of Oz after all. Only He was the man behind the curtain, sending forth smoke and mirrors and making promises He couldn't keep. Convinced the world of peace and security I had occupied for 27 years had been an illusion, night after night, I stood alone in the shower weeping, "Why me Lord?"

During the day, my work and family responsibilities kept me busy and somewhat distracted. But when darkness fell, so did my spirit. I felt helpless as if I were chained in a dungeon. I felt fear, doubt and despair like footfalls slowly descending the stairs to that cellar where I lay writhing in the face of the inevitable. In this confused condition, I became convinced I would never rebuild my life. Within this horror, I sensed a curtain being drawn by a wicked wind revealing an impostor conjuring the illusion of faith and hope. I wanted Jesus to heal me with a miracle like those recorded in the Gospels. It left me wondering if sadly His promises did not apply to me. And I wanted to know why.

"Whatever you ask in My name, that will I do" (John

14:13). *Really? That simply can't be true, Lord. I have begged you to lift my burden, but you don't. Every night the same old horror show replays in my mind, every single night …*

At times, that haunting question felt like the cruelest joke of all. I had been ravaged in that hotel room and left there a tattered remnant of my former self. I had dragged myself off the carpet of 939, returned home, and gotten on with my life, seeking to rediscover God and the joy of His fellowship. Yet, seemingly I was left empty with unanswered prayers, perhaps the greatest trial a child of God has to face. That's the question, isn't it, for believer and skeptic alike? The great English preacher, Oswald Chambers, said we are to expect these dark nights:

> *"Jesus said there are times when God cannot lift the darkness from you, but you should trust Him. At times God will appear like an unkind friend, but He is not; He will appear like an unnatural father, but He is not; He will appear like an unjust judge, but He is not. Keep the thought that the mind of God is behind all things strong and growing. Not even the smallest detail of life happens unless God's will is behind it."*

I believe that, but this thought brings scant comfort to one in the throes of the storm. I wish I had an answer to satisfy every doubting fiber in my soul, to bring even the most mocking atheist to Christ. But, I don't. I can only tell my story about how, through it all, I still trust Him.

Perhaps the place to start is a preliminary question. Just what did the Lord mean by statements like Matthew 7:7? Was He promising an "easy" button? Courage to the lion, a heart for the tin man, and a brain for the scarecrow?

To begin to find the answer, we must travel back in time to a cold, damp garden on the outskirts of first century Jerusalem. It is an especially dark night; the universe seems drained of love and hope. Fiends howl with joy, anticipating their greatest victory. There on His knees, sweat and blood pouring from His brow, the very Son of God pleads with His Father to take away His agony. His dearest friends lie sleeping a few feet away, while another "companion" betrays Him to those who plot to kill Him. A few hours later, after having been humiliated and flogged nearly to death, He will hang on a cross crying to His Father, "Why hast thou forsaken me?"

He had, of course, included one crucial qualification to His petition: *"Father, if it be Thy will, let this cup pass from me, but nevertheless not My will, but Thine be done"* (Luke 22:42). The cup did not pass; Jesus had to drink it to the bitter dregs. But, let's consider for a moment what would have happened had the Father answered differently. What Jesus feared most about going to the cross wasn't the physical torture, though it was horrendous. The real horror He faced was the tearing asunder of the Trinity – separation from the Father and the Spirit. There at Calvary, at the intersection of time and eternity – and who knows how long that awful moment really lasted – the perfect circle of love was shattered, the dance ended, and God experienced a broken heart we cannot begin to imagine.

But it was only for a time. What looked like the most tragic moment in time and eternity was actually the death knell of evil. The Trinity was restored, and our redemption assured. A prayer spoken not long before Gethsemane had been answered:

"... that they [we!] may be one, Father, just as you are in me and I am in you. May they also be in us" (John 17:21).

Had the cup passed, had Christ not fulfilled the mission for which He had come, none of us could ever fellowship with God. Love would have suffered devastating, cosmic, eternal, unfathomable defeat.

We are not God, you and I, but happy endings to stories we may never hear, at least not in this life, hang in the balance, depending on our obedience and faith when all seems lost. Our lives are intricately bound up with others, those we love and those we may never know. Pain and prayers that go unanswered remain a mystery, one I don't pretend to understand, but I do believe we find a clue in that lonely garden. If, as Isaiah, said *"By His stripes we are healed,"* I hope my story can provide a glimmer of hope to others. I want to be able to say as Joseph did to his brothers, who had sold him into slavery, *"You intended to harm me, but God meant it for good to accomplish what is now being done, the saving of many lives"* (Genesis 50:20).

In the meantime, however, I went most nights to my own Gethsemane, where tears were my only release. In the shower, I would weep and pray, pray and weep, my sobs muffled by the harsh spray which kept Mark and the girls from hearing my twisted cries as tears creased my face with the scalding water.

As I stepped from the shower, I patted the towel to my swollen eyes removing all evidence of my torment, allowing me to emerge from the bathroom a composed mom and wife, wearing that happy-go-lucky face.

During the Beth Moore Bible study concerning bondage, an overwhelming sense of discovery came to me: *"Do not be anxious about anything, but in every situation, by prayer and petition, with thanksgiving, present your requests to God. And the peace of God, which transcends all understanding, will guard your hearts and your minds in Christ Jesus"* (Philippians 4:6-7).

Those words from the apostle Paul are not a request; they are not conditional. They are a command, something we have to will to do in every situation. By the grace of God, if we refuse to be led by our feelings and instead lead them with our will, they will eventually follow. Think of it this way. How many of life's difficult tasks – exercise, yard work, even prayer – would you accomplish if you did them only when you felt like it? That's right, not much. Our emotions are an important part of our personalities, but they must serve the will. We simply cannot let our feelings determine the course of even so much as a day, but we have to work at it. Thanks be to God, He slowly but surely gave me strength to practice what Paul preached to the Philippians. As I got stronger, my mornings dawned a little brighter as I continued my battle with Satan.

With renewed strength, I had stepped closer to His power. His words leapt from the page into my soul, and I felt God's presence, even in the face of an attack. If only for a fleeting moment, He quieted my fears. Amid my hopelessness, I sensed He wanted a relationship with me. He said, *"Jenny Lynn, I can do nothing to change your past. But if you will walk with me, I will heal you."* Just as the Holy Spirit had touched my heart in Mrs. Beasley's Sunday School class, God assured me when the forces of anxiety seemed too strong and I was about to be overwhelmed, He would be my comforter, my restorer. He would guard me and never leave my side. As Christ, the great carpenter, put me back together piece by piece, I felt Jesus' easy yoke gently replace Satan's burdensome chains. As the sun began to rise in my valley of darkness, the Lord asked, *"Jenny Lynn, do you want light?"*

Yes, Lord.

With that I was blessed with a life-changing prayer in the Beth Moore Bible Study Guide: *"My child, I loved you before you were born. 'I knit you in your mother's womb' and knew what your first and last words would be. I knew every difficulty you would face. I suffered each one with you. Even the ones you didn't suffer with me. I had a plan for your life before you were born. The plan has not changed no matter what has happened or what you have done. You see, I already knew all things concerning you before I formed you. I would never allow any hurt to come into your life that I could not use for eternity. Will you let Me? Your truth is incomplete unless you view it against the backdrop of my Truth. Your story will forever remain half-finished ... until you let Me do My half with your hurt. Let Me perfect that which concerns you."*

After reading this prayer, God, in His masterful way further clarified a point for me. *"Jenny Lynn, your night of terror was not by My hand; therefore your life should no longer be defined by those 15 minutes. Peace will be with you when you return the responsibility of justice to Me."* But it was in His final and strongest commandment that He truly got my attention:

"You will remain imprisoned until you forgive your assailant."

15

Revelation

"But if you do not forgive others their sins, your Father will not forgive your sins." Matthew 6:15

It was in my seventh year of my journey to healing I realized the Christian life is joyful, but not without seasons of intense ambivalence. Jesus promises those who come to Him will find peace and joy. He says, *"My yoke is easy, and my burden is light"* (Matthew 11:30), and He keeps His promises. But salvation isn't the end of our struggle with doubt. The most committed believers find some of His commands difficult to obey. From a human perspective, they seem unreasonable, if not impossible. No sooner do we take those first faltering steps toward reconciliation with God, than we begin tripping over those stumbling blocks. Voices whisper echoes of the lie told in the Garden of Eden: "Did God really say ... ?" Even when we focus on His more comforting words, the ambivalence creeps in or in my case, God's words were difficult to grasp because I had not been "steeped" in the language of the Bible:

"Come to me, all you who are weary and burdened, and I will give you rest."

Yes, Lord. Rest. I am so tired. I'll gladly lay my burdens down, but what about ...?

"Be anxious for nothing ..."

Great! Uh ... Wait ... Anxious for nothing? Really? Nothing?

"Your heavenly Father knows all your needs"

Wonderful! I have a lot of those. You'll take care of them all? Of course, I should probably see about ... myself. I got that one covered, thank you.

"If you, then, though you are evil, know how to give good gifts to your children, how much more will your Father in heaven give good gifts to those who ask Him?"

I like the sound of that! Then again, there was the time I asked for...

"I will never leave you nor forsake you."

Praise the Lord! But, sometimes, Lord, I just don't feel You.

Then, there are those disquieting passages, the ones we "listen to but do not hear." On some level, maybe we think they don't really apply to us:

"Turn the other cheek."

What?

"You must take up your cross daily?"

Well, okay ... I think. Uh, just what does that mean exactly?

"But I tell you: Love your enemies and pray for those who persecute you."

Huh?

"But if you do not forgive others their trespasses ..."

You mean the ones who come crawling to us asking for pardon, right?

No, not really. Jesus didn't preface any of these commands with an if. He meant everything He said, and the moment He spoke to my heart about that last one, I knew I had to obey. But how? How could I forgive the man who had violated my very soul, who had shattered my peace, who had dragged me to the very precipice of hell itself? And what did that even mean?

Was I to behave as if the assault had never happened?

Was I to just let bygones be bygones?

Was I – God forbid – was I to somehow feel warm and fuzzy about this monster? Love my enemies! How in the world could I ever love him?

As is most always the case with obedience, the answer lies not with our feelings, but with our will. The Christian walk consists of two stages, salvation and sanctification. The first of these is immediate. We are saved the moment we accept Christ as Savior and Lord. Sanctification is one of those big "Church" words I have a hard time getting my brain around and actually have to look up in the dictionary time and time again. However, it is a life long process of conforming to Christ's character through obedience to his Word. God does not force anyone to believe in His Son. We must make that choice. People can choose to accept or reject God's love. But once we are saved, we mature in wisdom and truth only by obeying. Although nothing about God fits into neat, tightly defined categories, the order is usually something like this: First; we choose to obey. Second, we obey. Third, we come to the "Oh, I see" stage, where we understand what God was, after all, the *why* of His commands. If we *heed* His Word, it will bear the fruits of the Spirit which include love, joy and peace.

And so, convicted that I must be willing to forgive, I moved to the obedience stage. But wait. My invader had not left his calling card. Where is he? Is he alive? Is he dead? Here I was prepared to face the dark figure with God's commandment about forgiveness. But I had no address. So with renewed faith, I bowed my head and dialed up God, remembering his offering: *"Call to me and I will answer you and tell you great and unsearchable things you do not know"* (Jeremiah 33:3).

God answered, and I knew what to do. I walked to my file cabinet and located the police sketch of my assailant. Now with his face in front of me, I looked into the eyes of the one who had both glared at me as if I were not even a person and looked through me as if I were not really there, the fiend who took delight in destroying the good that had been my life to that point. While studying his daunting profile, I asked myself as I had so many times before, "What is the origin of rape and sexual assault?" They are about control, power and evil's beastly desire to dominate and desecrate. To the rapist, every victim is a symbol of the goodness and decency he has come to hate. He believes Satan who said goodness and decency are not for the likes of him. I began thinking about this derelict's way of life and how it was the polar opposite of mine. Surely his parents had not loved him or had been unable to love him. He had grown up amidst rampant crime and violence, envy and hatred, fear and suspicion. God's Spirit showed me how this man's ravaged mind had led him to do the unspeakable. These thoughts were really nothing more than my "fleshly" human way of conjuring up sympathy for the man so I might find it easier to forgive. But, God had to show me that, ultimately, forgiveness must begin with me and my obedience to Him.

God's insight led me to understand how seething anger metastasizes into hatred that eats away the soul and voids any chance at peace and happiness. And He reminded me again of that forsaken place called Golgotha where Jesus had uttered that unfathomable plea: "*Father forgive them for they know not what they do.*" The "them" in that petition included Jenny Lynn – and the man who had attacked me in Room 939. Christ died for all the sins of all of humanity for all of time, and it is not for us to make distinctions as to how severe a person's transgressions may be.

No sin is free; every one requires restitution. If I accidentally dent your car in the grocery store parking lot, justice says that it's only right that I pay for the repairs. Now, you could forgive the debt, but then either you drive a damaged vehicle or pay to have it fixed yourself. Either way, someone bears the burden. It doesn't simply disappear. Now that's a trivial example, of course, compared to the cosmic impact of all human sin. We cannot fathom what it cost God to allow His only Son to die on the cross, and those of us who accept that Jesus made that sacrifice for our sins have no right to deny it to another.

But God doesn't command us to forgive just to square all the accounts. Forgiveness heals us as much or more than it does those we pardon. You see, love cannot occupy the same space as hate or fear, causing an unforgiving heart to slowly shrink and shrivel into a hardened, callous mockery of love. In a cruelly ironic twist, we become like what we hate. We look upon our offenders as less than human, which, though much less in degree, is not really different in kind from the way the man in the hotel had looked upon me.

Does that mean that Jenny Lynn was gradually morphing into a fiend like that man? No. In the words of the Apostle Paul, *"May it never be!"* But every place in my heart unwilling to forgive was a space where love could not exist. Fear could reside in those dark spots. Anxiety and hate found themselves right at home there. But love and peace? No. The trauma and damage done to me that night were quite real. I needed God's healing in the worst way. Something terrible happened to me in that hotel room. I did nothing wrong that night! But the old Jenny Lynn couldn't really come back until I emptied my heart of the bitterness that had rooted so deeply there. I know now my decision not to forgive was the fuel that stoked the fire of the terror that ruled my life for so long. I had to forgive so that Jenny Lynn, the genuine Jenny Lynn, could come home again. C.S. Lewis wrote, *"Obedience is the road to freedom, humility the road to pleasure, unity the road to personality (our truest selves)."* Now with God's mighty power alive in me, I was convinced through His Word I could obey Him and forgive.

My pastor, Dr. John Waters, of First Baptist Church pronounced this challenge in a sermon:

Some don't want forgiveness ... forgive anyway!

Some can't ask for your forgiveness ... forgive anyway!

Some won't receive your forgiveness ... forgive anyway!

When I said aloud, "You are forgiven," I released my heavy burden to God and felt those chains of bondage falling from me, taking with them that 15-minute nightmare – my 20-year crucifixion. God could finally give me rest.

Now as I wait to pick up a daughter, move about my kitchen, or look through the windows onto my world, I am overcome with gratitude and awe as I think again of Jesus' dying words, *"It is finished"* (John 19:30).

Somehow I believe the man who attacked me is still out there. I hope and pray that he has heard our Lord's call and asked for forgiveness. I truly hope that he is at peace with God.

16

Almighty God

Many unbelievers – and believers, too – misunderstand the meaning of faith. They think it is blind superstition, a foolish, adolescent wish for a cosmic Santa Claus. But, think about those you trust the most, those in whom you place the most faith on a human level. I hope you have them in your life. Why do you trust them? Is it blind faith? Are they merely the projection of some childish fantasy? I doubt it. More likely, they have come through for you time after time. They have proven worthy of your trust. You *know* them. Hebrews Chapter 11 presents a tableau of faith, what is sometimes called the "Faith Hall of Fame." All those enshrined there including Abel, Abraham, Noah, and Moses, are considered champions of faith. Why? Because they *knew* God. He had proven trustworthy.

But this was ultimately my issue. Having left the church as a child, I had not learned to trust God. How could I? I didn't know Him. Consequently, when evil cast the shadow of death on me in Room 939 and every cold, hard fact in my life mocked the very idea of a loving, protective God, I floundered in a sea of unbelief, bitterly angry at the one who was supposed to be my Heavenly Father. To be honest, even the most committed, theologically sound Christian would struggle in the face of such an obscenity. That is neither a criticism of others, nor an excuse for my lack of faith. It is simply to say where I was spiritually after that night. But the rage and despair in my soul kept me from hearing His still small voice. In time, I would learn the comfort of fellowship with Him – in time, but for many years, I believed Satan's lies instead of God's promises.

I *believed* God could have and should have prevented the assault. Because He did not, I believed either He was powerless to help me or He did not care about me – or both.

The *truth* is He sent an angel to save me. He took that crumpled, damaged child into His bosom and began healing her the moment the man fled from that room, although it would be years before I would be able to see that.

I *believed* I was all alone.

The truth is He promised, *"Never will I leave you; never will I forsake you"* (Hebrews 13:5).

I *believed* my life would be easy if I was "good."

The truth is God never promised a life free of pain and suffering. Jesus told us to expect tribulation in this world, but that He would be with us in the midst of it.

I *believed* God made me powerless.

The truth is *"I can do all things through Christ who strengthens me"* (Philippians 4:13).

I *believed* God allowed me to lose my identity.

The truth is He gave me my truest self, the one hidden with Christ in God.

I *believed* God allowed me to become a victim.

The truth is *"I am more than a conqueror through Him who loves me"* (Romans 8:37).

I *believed* I would hurt forever.

The truth is "*By His stripes I am healed*" (Isaiah 53:4-5).

I *believed* Satan had destroyed me and I would never again be free from pain.

The truth is Christ "*redeems my life from the pit and crowns me with love and compassion*" (Psalm 103: 3-4).

I *believed* God allowed me to lose my way.

The truth is He *led me through the valley of the shadow of death, and now, that the waters are still, I can lie down in quiet and peace* (Psalm 23 paraphrased).

I *believed* I could do it alone.

The truth is the meek (teachable, remember?) shall inherit the earth.

I *believed* life wasn't worth living.

The truth is He was telling me "*See, I am doing a new thing! Now it springs up; do you not perceive it? I am making a way in the wilderness and streams in the wasteland*" (Isaiah 43:19).

I *believed* the invader would rule my life forever.

The truth is "*Greater is He who is in me than He who is in the world*" (I John 4:4).

But the grown woman who lay in pieces on the floor of Room 939 was in many ways still a child spiritually. She did not know these powerful truths. Had I not left church as a child, had I immersed myself in God's Word during all the intervening years, would I have gotten off that floor and been my old self in short order? Would the fear and anxiety have been powerless to hurt me? The answer is most emphatically, no. My life still would have been shattered. I'm sure I would have still been bitterly angry with God. I would have still faced a cataclysmic struggle to hold onto my faith.

But I know one fact for certain. Evil's lies stand no chance against the sword of the Spirit. They still come at me with ferocity, and sometimes my knees buckle just a little, but I do not fall. I wield that mighty weapon in one hand and the shield of faith in the other. When spiritual war came to me, I was not ready. Now, I have learned to fight and fight well, and I know when I left the church many years ago, God knew what I would face. Even then He said to me as He had to the disobedient people of Israel centuries before Christ's birth,

"Do not fear, for I have redeemed you;
I have summoned you by name; you are mine.
When you pass through the waters,
I will be with you;
and when you pass through the rivers,
they will not sweep over you.
When you walk through the fire,
you will not be burned;
the flames will not set you ablaze.
For I am the LORD your God,
the Holy One of Israel, your Savior" (Isaiah 43: 1b-3).

God had always known every detail of what life had in store for me – Room 939 and, before that fateful night, the years of living with my Mother's addiction to alcohol – and He had purposed all along to bring me through those fiery trials with my soul intact.

Like many other parents in the 1960s and 70s, my mother and father drank socially. They partied with their crowd, sometimes even during the week, but went faithfully to work the next morning and never neglected their parental duties. A rock-solid duet, Mom and Dad loved us and reared us with honorable values. They took an interest in everything Janna and I did and demonstrated unwavering support as they watched their daughters participate in various activities including basketball, track, cheerleading, and even one-act plays. We never looked through disappointed eyes at empty seats where our parents should have been. As Janna and I grew older and talked about our dreams, our parents always listened to our plans and encouraged us to go for it. They cherished their daughters, and we knew it.

But all was not perfect. I remember how Mama and her colleagues enjoyed a toddy in the back of her law office after hours. These afternoon delights seemed perfectly normal to me. But somewhere along the way, the social drinking became something different for my mother. Alcohol, which in the beginning had been a stress reducer after a hard day's work, became the glue that held her together, while simultaneously breaking her apart. By the time I entered high school, I knew her drinking had become more than social. It was taking our mother away from Janna and me. Many a night, I lay in bed wanting to move to the pantry and rid our home of the Seagram's 7 Whiskey.

I would visualize unscrewing the cap to all those brown bottles and watching the poison swirling into darkness, in the process washing away the pall that had descended upon our home. When Mama drank, I saw the hurt and sadness in her eyes; I knew something powerful had taken hold of her. My strong mother faced an enemy she didn't know how to defeat. But as a child, I had no right to remove the liquor from our home, and I lacked the courage to discuss the issue with anyone – not even my sister. Janna and I kept quiet, knowing – and fearing – that one day our Mother's drinking would take her to the brink of an abyss where we might lose her. Now, I think that perhaps the slow, steady grind of those anxious days planted the seeds of the anxiety that would seize control of me many years later. Cataclysmic trauma can shatter one's heart in a moment, but the drip, drip, drip of a steadily growing specter like alcoholism in the home can do tremendous damage, too.

Janna and I truly admired this maverick who blazed trails and made the notion of women attorneys more respected and legitimate. We were proud of this champion who went to night law school in Atlanta at the age of 21. On July 11-12, 1956, 361 took the Georgia State Bar Examination with my mother being one of 83 candidates who passed. This dirt farmer's daughter proved success comes to those who persevere. Before the days of Pell Grants, low-interest student loans, and "entitlements," she earned every step of her way to the glass ceiling, becoming Bulloch County's first female attorney and 22 years later, Georgia's first Governor-appointed female Superior Court Judge. Years later, knowing what she had sacrificed and how hard she worked at her craft, Janna and I remained committed to her and stood by her side, whether she was sober or intoxicated. She was still our mom, the bravest and most accomplished woman we knew. We had *faith* in her because of all the times she had come through for us.

While Janna and I enjoyed college life, we would often call home and talk to Mom about sorority life, football weekends and oh yeah, how we were doing with our class work. During these conversations, we began to realize that alcohol had tightened its grip on her. Her sometimes incoherent responses confirmed Mother was in trouble. Moreover, her memory lapses revealed she also suffered periodic blackouts, a clear danger signal. Things really began falling apart my junior year when I realized Mother was beginning to drink not only at night, but also on occasion during the day. However despite her descent into alcoholism, she never missed a session of court. She was revered by her peers as a professional who was passionate about law, especially when it involved children, by protecting their rights in domestic cases. She had an impeccable work record, exemplary in every way.

Nevertheless, her drinking loomed as an increasingly dangerous issue. Remarkably, many drinkers can function at very high levels. Alcoholics can be amazingly resourceful, and this affliction often affects the especially bright, motivated, and conscientious among us. Consequently, they manage to "keep it together," at least on the outside, but internally, as their addiction eats at them, the façade begins to crumble. So it was with Mama.

Eventually, drinking began compromising her principles. Finally, on April 11, 1983, a representative of the court system contacted Daddy to express concern about Mother's condition. Late that same afternoon, we drove Mom to the office of Dr. Albert "Buster" Deal, our family physician. Having stayed after hours, Nurse Doris Cannon and Dr. Albert were waiting in the office. Nothing about this "appointment" felt normal. We moved through the back door quietly. Standing in the nurses' station where I had gotten immunizations to ward off everything from polio to rubella and measles, Dr. Albert cut to the chase with one of the most disturbing, uncomfortable deliverances which still resonates in my mind.

"Faye," he said," I believe you've got a problem and need help."

"No, Dr. Albert, I believe you're the one who has the problem here."

"Faye, you need to go to Willingway Hospital."

"No."

"Well, I'll admit you to the Bulloch County Hospital."

"You will not."

"Okay then Faye, I'll bring you to my home and you can stay with Helen and me."

She wouldn't budge. "No."

When he next mentioned a treatment center in St. Simons Island, Mama relented and said, "Okay, I'll go there." And I finally exhaled in relief, but only for a moment. Then it hit me – my Mama was about to be admitted to a sterile, clinical environment too far away from home.

At this point, she said very little. Even in her angry defiance, my mother knew the truth – her honored position as a judge could end if she did not heed Dr. Albert's advice. And so, this kind, wonderful woman whom we all loved and looked up to had received a "sentencing" of her own. Now, of course, I see God's hand on the situation. Those awkward moments in Dr. Albert's office had not been a trial ending in punishment, but rather one of those moments of grace when God gently takes us by the hand and leads us to a place of healing.

In less than an hour, Mama had her bags packed. She remained quiet during our long journey to St. Simons, where Daddy and I admitted her into Charter by the Sea. At midnight, I watched her leave my side and walk into the detox unit. I had no idea what was beyond those doors. Hope? Recovery? I just knew I wanted my Mama back. Returning to the car in the darkness, I searched the sky for a bright star, a hopeful harbinger of healing. But it was a very cloudy night.

Back home in Statesboro, I cried myself to sleep with this petition: "God please bring Mama back to me. I still need her." Little did I know how very much I would need her in the coming years when, like her, I would descend into a very dark place with no stars in sight.

17

For He Waits

When Daddy, Janna and I returned to Charter three weeks later for family counseling sessions, one look at Mom told us she was a changed woman. She greeted us in the parking lot with a glowing look of clarity beaming from her eyes. She was healthy and relaxed. The judge was back.

A week later, her treatment completed, Faye Sanders Martin walked from Charter and began her journey of sobriety that now approaches 30 years. I looked on proudly as my Mother once again lived with the passion, grit, and undying devotion to her family and her profession.

As a recovering alcoholic, Mother drew on her experience with the disease and her rehabilitation to offer hope to others who suffered from this and other debilitating addictions. She was the mother I had known all my life, a lady of pride and dignity. Only now she had increased in wisdom and compassion. During her 55-year career as an attorney and judge, she would be honored with numerous commendations and awards recognizing her service to the bench, bar, and public.

Jenny Lynn, however, still did not have the eyes to see her own need for God's grace. I remained steadfastly self-reliant, definitely not in line to inherit the wealth of the "meek." Never once during the next seven years did I call on Him for His power until that dark November night in Room 939. Even after returning to church that Sunday morning when I felt His presence in our bedroom, I struggled with my faith many years before finally taking His Word into my heart and becoming truly His. We had been attending church faithfully for six years when, in 1996, God set in motion one of His plans to awaken my slumbering spirit and bring this stubborn lost sheep back into the fold. He used some Godly disciples for that deliverance. Undoubtedly, He chose Wayne Brannen, Lindsay Walker and Kathy Rushing, team teachers of my Sunday School class, to lift the scales from my eyes. Additionally, our Pastor, George Daunhauer, confirmed His Word from the pulpit.

Until this point in my life, the Holy Spirit had been a casual acquaintance. But all that changed as His Word stirred the nearly cold embers in my heart and kindled a new passion for my role as a wife and mother. Our church's mid-week Bible study sessions complemented my awakening and fed my hunger for the Word.

I can describe this transformation as nothing other than a miracle. His Scripture initially made very little sense to me. How could it? My Bible had collected a lot of dust in the years following my departure from church, but with renewed interest, I realized what a treasure trove it was. The depth and texture of this Holy Book inspired me each time I opened it to seek His guidance.

With my brothers and sisters in Christ guiding me, eager anticipation and thirst to know Him overpowered the embarrassment I felt at my ignorance of Scripture. Ironically, a children's Bible with descriptive pictures and graphics became a favorite edition. I guess I needed to pick up where I had left off at the age of eight. My blue bookmark grew worn and tattered as I moved it from Genesis to Exodus, and then into the New Testament with Paul's epistles. It even spent some time in Revelation (I'm still confused about that one!) That old bookmark fits most comfortably in the Gospels, though, as the Man whose story they tell leaps from those pages each time I open them, always amazing me. I'll definitely never take the Lord for granted again. I close this chapter with these reminders:

It's never too soon to have a relationship with God. *For He waits.*

It's never too late to have a relationship with God. *For He waits.*

At the age of 36, I was thankful God was patient and had waited for me.

18

Reversal

In 1999, I realized just how thoroughly I had isolated myself from most of my dearest friends, the people who could have fed my soul the most and helped me recover my truest self. I had become a most unnatural being, a quiet, withdrawn Jenny Lynn.

I had cut others out of my life, at least in part, due to the way the community responded to my sexual attack. We rarely know what to say to someone in the throes of tragedy.

I know how you must feel. *No. We can't know how another feels in these situations.*

Time heals all. *Sorry. I'm sure that's true, but it just doesn't help a whole lot right now.*

I love you. Please let me know what I can do to help. *This one helps, of course, but how can someone reeling in alternating states of pain and numbness answer that question?*

When nothing seems the right approach, most people probably revert to that old standby: denial. I knew their thinking was "If we don't discuss it, it never happened." It was too much for even the most caring and empathic to handle. Of course, that attitude only made the 300-pound gorilla loom even larger in the room. Then there were those few, especially ones like cousin Jone, my "noticer" and "listener" who endlessly chipped away at the barriers

I had erected. As they tried to meet me head on and remain engaged, I effectively frustrated their efforts. And so, for years I lived alienated, not only from those dearest to me, but also from myself. How could I love others as myself when I didn't even recognize the self I had become? I had always moved with grace and spontaneity; now my every move was halting and tentative. Whereas the old Jenny Lynn, the true original, never passed a rose she didn't stop and savor, the timid shadow who had taken her place greeted glorious sunrises and grey, foggy mornings with the same torpid indifference. The laughter of children no longer seemed like echoes of heaven's choirs, but faded instead into just another background noise. The Jenny Lynn who never let a conversation lapse into pregnant pauses became reticent, lacking the energy to enliven those around her. I longed for the time when I could stand in line with friends, chatting excitedly as we waited to see a movie. I wanted to relish the atmosphere of an outdoor concert or enjoy a grand art exhibition.

But it was not to be. The free-spirited butterfly of my being crawled back into its cocoon, preferring the safety of dormancy to the dangers of flight. I still had my wings, but they had atrophied.

I left Room 939 with a changed view of the world. I no longer considered it safe, and our culture, saturated with violence, only made things worse. I may have been indifferent to life's simple beauties, but I noticed every movie rife with graphic rape scenes, profanity, and inhumanity. Even television invaded our homes with indecency and coarseness. How could I relax when every medium of entertainment conjured images of that night in Atlanta? I lived in a different world than did those who had never been damaged by the trauma of an assault. Others may have seen the moral cesspool of popular culture and fretted about where we might be headed. I saw society already plunging into the abyss.

I no longer sought opportunities to help others. Instead I felt powerless, misshaped, and ill-defined. But even then, I knew in the depths of my soul that I was being told a lie. Somehow, I had to dig my bloody fingers deeper into the ledge where I held on to a faint glimmer of hope. In the face of all this despair, I could still hear traces of His voice.

> *Take my hand, Jenny Lynn. I will pull you up. You're still the woman I created you to be. We've just got to peel away that cocoon you've wrapped around yourself. It's just a web of lies and fear. Love and fear cannot occupy the same space, Jenny Lynn.*

So, I held on, vigilantly searching for any glimmer of that old spark. I longed for the spontaneous child and teenager who loved music and the theater. As a child, I constantly orchestrated performances with my friends as actors. Every family or neighborhood gathering included an original Jenny Lynn production. I was writer, producer, director, and set designer. I assembled crews, taught my friends how to move on stage and brought out their inner star with my deft touch. All the world was indeed a stage when Jenny Lynn was around.

When I was nine, I attended a Donny Osmond concert and knew for sure he had crooned "Puppy Love" just for me. My sister and I cruised the record store downtown several times a week to buy the latest hit tunes. How well I remember those 45 rpm discs for 99 cents. Music filled our bedrooms and our souls with the rhythms of the day. We kept Georgia Power in business with our turntables spinning 24/7. It didn't take long for the smooth vinyl of our records to become a distorted maze of scratches as we constantly dropped the needle unmercifully on the turntable (Younger readers can google this strange word.) as over and over, we sang and swayed to the beat of Michael Jackson, David Cassidy, the Beatles, and the Monkees. If IPods had been around in those days, we might never have come up for air.

My penchant for putting on a show continued in high school. Our creative juices inspired by a blend of hormones and imagination, my girlfriends and I devised elaborate dance routines that we considered great artistry. Without a doubt, *Grease* was our most spectacular home spun performance. During the summer of 1978, Janna, Beth Brannen, Sandra Thackston, Pam Newton, Jessica Johnston, Becky Newton and I made up the cast and crew that brought this production, live and in color, to an audience of our parents and their friends at the Coast House on Colonel's Island.

We labored for days that summer on our command performance for the Coast crowd. I remember the delighted looks on the adults' faces when we came to the part of "Born to Hand Jive," and our slender, teenaged, uninhibited bodies went down to the ground in unison while screaming, "How low can you go, how low you can go." That close-knit group of adults went wild. It confirmed we were beautiful and totally in tune. Sweating and strutting our stuff like Tina Turner, we brought the house down and rekindled memories of when they, too, had "cut loose." Actually, they probably said "cut a rug." We were from "God's Country," good ole Southern girls with the spunk and daring to unabashedly display our talents. Unhindered by the awkwardness and self-consciousness that can bedevil teenagers, we felt completely at ease in the spotlight. I was in my element there, although not in an egotistical way. I do admit to loving the attention, but I more than that, I loved entertaining people and seeing them enjoy themselves. I wanted to bring everyone into my world, to a place where they felt as at home as I did. Little did I know that a few years later, I would be ripped from that world myself.

After Room 939, I wandered for nine years in a desert where my existence seemed like an unending, ill-fitting anxiety attack. It was as if I had been beamed into "Bizarro World" of the old Superman comics where everything was a perverse reversal of the normal. Oddly, however, though I could not have articulated these thoughts at the time, the spirit of an old hymn resonated somewhere deep inside me:

> *"Whatever my lot, Thou has taught me to say, It is well, it is well, with my soul."*

I will never forget the moment when God said to the storm that raged around me, "Peace! Be Still!" I was in Barnes and Noble Bookstore looking for the newest bestseller in the "Self-Help" section. I was convinced if I read enough inspirational books, I would find that one that would give me just the answer I needed, the key that would enable Jenny Lynn to fix herself. Yes, I was still convinced I could fix myself. After all, isn't that why they call it "*Self* Help"? I have always been a highly disciplined person. Once I commit to something, I am in it for the long haul. As a case in point, I started lifting weights 11 years ago. Since that time I have seldom missed my "date" with my workout partner Dawn Oliver. Religiously, I have met Dawn on Mondays and Fridays at 8:30 a.m. to exercise with a personal trainer. I believed I could discipline my soul just as I had my body. I could go it alone. Why not? By that time, I had been "alone" for quite some time, despite the loving husband, family, and friends who surrounded me.

I had read *The Last Lecture, Who Moved my Cheese, The Five Love Languages: How to Express Heartfelt Commitment to Your Mate,* and many more. After leafing through texts on mental health and emotional despair, I turned into the aisle of the "Religion" section, and then I had one of those epiphanies, again not some esoteric secret of the universe, but rather a sudden insight to the shining truth that had been right there in front of me for so long. My eyes fell on the myriad translations of the Bible that lined those shelves, and I had to ask myself some obvious questions:

Jenny Lynn, how long have you been back in the church now? Who do you say God is? So, why exactly have you been seeking wisdom from all these human authors? If you believe the Bible is God's Word, then don't you think it's about time you really took it to heart? Did you really think all those human authors know more than God? Blessed are the who? Oh yeah, the teachable.

For years, I had sought every so-called authority in Self-Help to repair me, but I had missed the point: the only bestselling Author I needed was God. It was time to walk with the Lord and really get to know Him. He had sustained me in my torment for nine years, but now it was time for me to step deeper into my relationship with Him, to really trust Him. At that moment of quiet revelation, His mercy and goodness covered me, and I finally began to see though the prodigal Jenny Lynn had turned into the lane leading home, she had yet to really let her Father embrace her and welcome her back to the fold.

My restoration didn't begin that day in the bookstore. What began that Sunday morning when I told Mark we were going back to church was real. But growth in grace is a long and uneven process of learning to trust Him, interspersed here and there with a quantum leap of faith. I took a leap that morning. I began to truly "let go and let God." Fear didn't disappear that day. In fact, I will have to fight every day as I let God renew my mind and transform me. But the liar lost a major battle in those moments of insight. *He would return again and again, but he would never find my house swept clean, only to be left empty because I began to furnish it with the truth* (Matthew 12:44). I wouldn't swear to it now so many years later, but I think I may have stopped by the CD aisle before I left the store. Maybe I even did a little "hand jive" as I walked to my car. And I'm sure it wasn't long before I dialed up some of my girlfriends to arrange a night at the movies.

19

Down Time

By 2005, I had reconnected with my friends, adding the richness and texture to my life that had gone missing for most of the previous decade. As my faith grew stronger, so did my resolve to overcome the timidity that had made me so unrecognizable to myself and to those who knew and loved me best. The face who returned my glance in the mirror began to look more familiar. I was healing.

But all those years of smiling through the pain, of crying in the shower only to emerge the brave cheerful wife and mama had taken their toll. We all experience dry spells, even if only briefly, when we must force ourselves to be upbeat on the outside when, on the inside, we feel like dying. We do this for the sake of those we love, but the cost to our psyche can be devastating. We open our front door to the world, greeting it with a smile, while simultaneously keeping one hand behind us to force back the sadness straining to peek over our shoulder. It is mentally and spiritually exhausting, and the consequences creep up on us stealthily. In my case, a new acquaintance had entered the picture, one with whom I had nothing in common, but who insisted on being my constant companion.

From the outset, she made me uneasy. She never smiled, she wore no bright colors, she disdained the sunshine, preferring instead the clammy wetness of a rainy day, and she favored the melancholy sounds of lament over the stirring rhythms of praise and thanksgiving. She erected a stronghold in my life. Her presence cast a pall on the light that had begun to break through the clouds of my bout with PTSD. Whereas fear and anxiety surged through me and kept me perpetually on the edge of a precipice, this new intruder painted everything in a tedious, life-sapping grey. She posed perhaps the greatest threat I had faced since Room 939. With her around, I slowly slipped into an apathetic torpor. The longer she remained in my life, the closer I came to a numb resignation. If I couldn't chase her away, I risked living out my days as a hollow shell. As Douglas McArthur once said of the old soldier, I would "just fade away." I wouldn't cry a lot, I wouldn't hurt as deeply perhaps, but I would never really smile again either.

Her effect on me became even more apparent as I increased my involvement in church and community service. These activities should have brought me to life, but instead I approached them as tedious, perfunctory tasks. My new companion was ever-present – lurking about as I prepared dinner, reviewed my daughters' class projects and worked in marketing our newly established business, Joiner-Anderson Funeral Home. No matter how fulfilling my pace, she was there. Even as I lay my head on the pillow, I knew she would be waiting for me when the morning sun gleamed through our bedroom curtains.

This stranger had such a deep foothold that it wasn't until a beautiful spring day in 2009 that I finally saw her identity.

Her name was Depression.

While I had marshaled my forces to fight the fear and anxiety head on, she had snuck in from the rear and attacked an unguarded spot in my spirit and established an undeniable authority. I no longer read fiction. Mystery, romance, and intrigue no longer moved me. Why should they? I didn't believe in happy endings anymore. I stopped listening to music, not so much because it failed to cheer me. Instead, I think I just forgot to turn it on. Whenever I started to daydream, my secret companion would give me that, "What for? You know dreams don't come true" look!

I began to shut myself off from my friends once again. It simply took too much energy to share their joys or their heartaches, and I cared nothing for small talk. I just didn't care to be involved. Lady Depression took control. I wanted to disappear. I struggled to maintain my roles as a loving mother and wife, and to stay connected to God, but I really just wanted to lie down and make it all go away. I was tired of fighting; every part of me wanted to surrender.

As I stood on my patio looking into the depths of the beautiful woods surrounding our home, I wasn't yet so void of feeling that I couldn't cry. Tears filled my eyes as I noted the beautiful paths I once walked. For a moment, I almost let myself believe they still led to new and exciting places. Then, I glanced over at my somber companion.

You'll just set yourself up for more disappointment, you know. How many times have you thought you had this thing licked? You never did! That's right; you always end up back in the same place. Hope always disappoints. Don't you see that?

She lied, of course, but I lacked the strength to lift the sword against her. If I had, Paul's exhortation to the Romans would have sent her scurrying in defeat. He told them that "*suffering produces perseverance; perseverance, character; and character, hope. And hope does not put us to shame, because God's love has been poured out into our hearts through the Holy Spirit, who has been given to us"* (Romans 5: 3-5). But I just didn't have the fight in me to act on Paul's commands, so with a sigh, I agreed with the deceiver and went back inside.

Somehow, though, I managed to soldier on and hide my sadness from Mother, Janna, Mark, and the girls. I thought it was what I needed to do for their sake. An emissary from the Father of Lies, Lady D maneuvered me into a conspiracy of silence and convinced me to keep up a normal, happy facade. Already running on fumes, little did I know this was the worst approach I could have taken. Captured in her game, tragically I became the actress this demon dame desired.

On Easter Sunday 2009, our extended family gathered at our home for the annual Anderson egg hunt. The children were running around the yard, their legs carrying them swiftly from tree branch to water fountain, their squeals of delight filling the air. My brothers-in-law and sisters-in-law stood on the back porch peeling the boiled eggs and flavoring them with salt and pepper. A beautiful symphony suffused this special day – laughter, playful banter, delightful notes of discovery, and all the vibrant sounds of a Southeast Georgia spring.

Yet more than anything else, amidst a loving family, one of God's greatest blessings, on the day we celebrate the happiest of all endings, I wanted them all to go away. I kept looking at my watch thinking, *Can I survive these people on my porch for two more hours?* I wanted to scream and run or sneak away into the background. It had been absolute drudgery to drag out Easter baskets, spread tablecloths, prepare the snacks and drinks, and most of all to dig deep within and find that happy face, plaster it on and pretend to celebrate this egg hunt.

I sat there trying to engage these joyful people in their joyful world, yet all I could feel was the dull, aching sadness of lost hope as the specter of the dark lady lurked nearby. Then I would beat myself up as if it were simply a matter of choosing not to be sad.

Jenny Lynn ... you have everything in the world you need for happiness ... two healthy children, a husband who loves you, a family who cares for you, a beautiful home, gorgeous clothes, ten million shoes ... look at your backyard and take it all in ... a pool with sparkling blue water, a paradise you and Mark created to share with your family and friends. And all you can think about is the fact you're still not happy!

But Janna's keen eyes knew something wasn't right. Sensing the presence of my silent companion, she leaned in and whispered, "Jenny Lynn, are you okay? You seem so quiet today." As I looked into the eyes of my sister who had teased me unmercifully as a child for wearing "granny panties," with whom I had watched endless hours of *Gilligan's Island* and swum in the Ogeechee River, the sister with whom I had always been able to share anything and not be judged – I lied: "Janna, I'm just a little tired today." She didn't buy it but knew pressing the issue would do no good.

For 15 years, I had fought hard against fear and anxiety. I had learned to wield the sword of God's Word. I had claimed the victory Christ won at Calvary and sealed on Resurrection Sunday. I had felt His presence that Sunday morning that brought me back to church after all those years. My Bible study with my sisters in Christ had renewed me. I had experienced yet another awakening in the bookstore, one that had restored some of my zest for life. So, why had none of it lasted? Was it all a cosmic joke? The lady in black said it was. She murmured more poison into my ear: "Wouldn't it be easier just to give up? You deserve a rest. Stop the fighting. See through the illusion into the truth. Live out your days in 'quiet desperation.'"

That's often what depression feels like: quiet desperation that dissolves into numb resignation. But God was not finished with me. He had taught me to "soar on wings like eagles" and to "run and not grow weary," but I had yet to learn to *"walk and not be faint"* (Isaiah 40:31). God gives us those transfiguring mountaintop experiences, but we spend most of our days walking in the demon-possessed valley where disillusionment and discouragement can blur the vision if we are not careful.

I nearly did just that; I came perilously close to losing heart. Please don't misunderstand. It is my prayer my story touches the hearts of those who hurt and who may also be close to giving up; and I don't want to leave the impression our bouts with depression and despondency always result from lack of faith or some "unconfessed sin." Depression is real. It can result from a myriad of causes – the long erosive battering of PTSD, a chemical imbalance in the brain, even heredity. It is most certainly not a sign of weakness. Depression is an affliction, and it attacks good people, strong people. As God uses many resources to heal us, faith is the foundation that undergirds them all.

Therefore, despite the victories He had won for me, I still had much to learn about walking with God. He still had much to teach me about faith and patience. I had to stop laying my burden down at the foot of the cross only to come back and pick it up again. If we depend on our own strength to fix whatever is wrong in our lives, we will run dry, but God's supply is inexhaustible. It is just that for a while, I forgot to draw from it.

Always on the lookout for a miracle cure, I noticed

an impressive national advertising campaign for a new antidepressant. As a marketing professional, I thought, "Wow! That commercial is a winner." It followed the basic rules I had preached over and over during my marketing career. A sales pitch must distill into a simple, compelling message. The average commercial viewer's attention span equals about one flutter of a hummingbird's wings, so "catch phrases" have only an instant to work. Declare the name of the product within the first 10 seconds of the commercial and include sound effects that complement the spiel. And by all means offer a money-back guarantee. I was right as the ad campaign later garnered an 'All-Stars Large Pharma Marketing Team' award from Medical Marketing & Media.

But these pharmaceutical pitches must also include all possible side effects: "New or worsening depression symptoms, unusual changes in behavior, thoughts of suicide, agitation, panic attacks, aggressiveness, restlessness, or hyperactivity. You may experience headaches, weakness, confusion, memory problems, or feel unsteady." These caveats sounded innocuous, however, when compared to the demonic life overpowering me. The possibility of a quick fix sounded awfully tantalizing.

Still I was conflicted as a sampling of my inner dialogue and prayers reveals: Imprisoned in my hideout from the demon named depression, I closed my eyes and said to myself, *Think Jenny Lynn. Think. How can **you** find the way back to the life you once lived?*

In the next moment, I turned to God and said, *"Dear Lord, come to my rescue and release me from this madness."* As I uttered this plea, I remembered the words of the psalmist: *"Yet I am always with you; you hold me by my right hand"* (Psalm 73:23). As before, when I turned to my

Heavenly Father, I experienced quiet and serenity. But who did I really think was going to heal me, God or Jenny Lynn?

We're all familiar with the old saying, "God helps those who help themselves," or more specifically, God helps those who realize they cannot fix themselves. He cannot work with us when we choose to remain steadfastly self-sufficient. It's basically what happened in Eden when Adam and Eve in effect said to God, "This is such a beautiful place you've built. Perfect climate, sex in paradise – who could ask for more? So, thanks, we'll take it from here." We all know how that turned out.

So to truly find and experience God's rest, we must yield our all to Him. Little did I know at this time of my life, God had already written the prescription for my healing process through His disciples, Drs. Jack Rainer, Carla Branch and Ellen Emerson.

Our Great Physician is a loving and patient God. How do I know that? He never left my side during my "down" time as He waited for the moment I accepted His prescription, trusted Him and looked "up."

20

The Truth

It's a dilemma all caring parents face. We want our children to grow up in a world of joy and wonder, yet we know how hard reality bites sometimes, and sooner or later (nowadays, it's usually sooner) our kids will catch more than a glimpse of life's dark underbelly. Reports of terrorism, natural disasters, and economic turmoil abound in the media. The information highway teems with exit ramps to all manner of dangers. Even the most vigilant parents can't shelter their children from the onslaught of disturbing imagery that floods our world. Still we try to shield them as best we can, knowing we won't completely succeed. So, we must choose how much to tell them about life's unpleasant inevitabilities – and when to begin drawing back that curtain. Should we vaccinate our kids with small doses of reality so they can build a resistance? How do we alert them to life's unavoidable dangers all the while teaching them to hope and dream and that we live in good world created by a perfect God?

All parents face these tough questions, but what in the world do you do when you have a story like mine to tell? I knew the moment I found out I was to be a mother I would one day have to tell my children about the nightmare in 939. I prayed for the right time and the right place – and for the right words. I wanted to assure them the God Mark and I worshiped would protect them and guide them, if only they would trust Him.

But you can see the horns of my dilemma, can't you? How could I make them aware of evil, yet enable them to feel safe and secure when I wrestled with so many doubts myself – when I had so often stumbled blindly through the valley, when life with God had been such a stomach-churning roller coaster ride? I did not want fear to control their lives as it had mine for so long, but neither did I want them to enter adulthood unaware they have an adversary who roams about seeking ways to devour them (I Peter 5:8). After all, one of Satan's most effective strategies is to convince people he doesn't exist.

Thankfully, God sent the words I needed when giving Morgan and Allison tough, practical advice: "As you leave the nest, relax and savor God's good gifts, but take nothing for granted. Always let your instincts and your good sense guide you. Wherever you are or whatever you're doing, if you get that strange feeling, go the other way. Be 'street smart.'" Later, as I thanked God for getting me through those revelations, I added one more plea: "Father, watch over them; let them live freely and openly, loving you and claiming your promise to give them rest and peace when their lives get hard and confusing."

Telling Morgan about the incident proved to be non-climactic. Because she is our pragmatist, a "tell me like it is" kind of girl who meets life head on, I had little trouble planning our talk. We were sitting on the patio, discussing life, the past, the present, the future, when the Spirit gently let me know the time was right. Calm and composed, Morgan listened as I told her of my experience that terrible night, sparing none of the gruesome details. I held her hand tightly and gave her a Mother's advice. Although outwardly I matched her calm demeanor, inwardly my nerves sizzled with that old familiar charge of angst because I knew she would soon be old enough to drive and venture into the world without Mama's vigilant eye to watch over her. Even quick errands to the nearby grocery, not to mention weekend trips to the beach with friends, would soon run my anxiety meter to a full ten. Nevertheless, I thank God that what she heard that day did not shake Morgan's confidence and resolve. She is a determined and focused young woman with her eyes set steadfastly on her goals.

My talk with Allison proved to be much more emotional and cathartic. Although I had planned and rehearsed just the right approach, a sudden surge of panic forced me to broach the subject in a context I had not imagined. Allison is more sensitive, so I wanted to be extra prepared for her reaction. But it was her response to something else I said that forced me to have the conversation at such an unexpected moment. In November 2010, we went shopping in Savannah, our minds set on fun and frivolity. Ever since 939, November had always been especially difficult for me. While the advent of the holiday season filled most with eager anticipation and warm nostalgia, I would begin to feel a strong undertow of sadness and loss, as if the anniversary of a loved one's death was approaching. In a symbolic way, I suppose that's what it was. I have never questioned other PTSD sufferers about how they feel when circumstances of time or place awaken memories of their trauma, but I imagine they experience similar onslaughts of fear and dread, knowing an old nemesis is about to come calling yet again. Like me, they "fear the fear" and grow anxious about the anxiety. Always hyper-vigilant, they ratchet up the intensity and double the guard. The dull ache in the pit of their stomachs signals the return of torment.

On that November day, however, I managed to shove all the foreboding into the background of my consciousness – only not as deep as I thought. As Allison and I parked in front of Home Goods with all of Savannah spread before us, I thought of only one thing: shopping! Then suddenly, with my guard down, fear struck me, and I changed – like so many times before – from survivor into victim. A black man wandered aimlessly toward us, and despite 20 years of inuring myself to such a commonplace scene, I fell apart as this "threat" provoked a PTSD-induced Pavlovian response. As Allison moved to open the door, I hit the locks and whispered, "Allison, that man doesn't look right. Let's just stay here for a few minutes until he is gone."

Immediately, my 15-year-old made a shocking remark: "Mama, you're *such* a racist!" Stunned by my daughter's degrading reaction, I felt nothing but sadness; I never dreamed a child of mine would consider me a bigot. From the time they were old enough to understand, I had carefully taught them to be color-blind. Mark and I brooked no bigotry of any kind, racial, religious, or otherwise. So as Allison had seen only the brave, composed mother, now she had come face to face with the victim of 939. There we sat, my daughter confused and angry, her mother hurt and bewildered.

Black people weren't always my bane. In fact, outside my family, the person I loved most as a child was an African American. From the time I was a baby until my tenth birthday, Bessie Burns Grimes blessed my life with her angelic presence. Bessie was my mother while my Mom worked. As she moved from room to room dusting, washing clothes or preparing a meal, there I would be in my portable cradle just a few steps away from her watchful eye, while in soft tones she reminded me, "You're Bessie's good baby." She saw me through chicken-pox, one-sided mumps, a tonsillectomy and every stomach virus known to humankind. Bessie would pull double duty when Janna and I would often get sick at the same time. Unfailingly, Bessie would hover over us, taking temperatures, applying suppositories (Now, that's love!), and measuring doses of medicines. She nursed us back to health with the gentle touch of a true healer. When pin worms beset us, Bessie dutifully washed the sheets in scalding water. When we threw up, she always took care of business, with never a word of complaint.

Bessie loved us dearly and sacrificed for us as if we were her own children – unconditionally, but not without some ground rules, especially as we grew older. She wasn't going to let her girls grow up pampered and spoiled. We weren't going to loll on the veranda, calling for more iced-tea and some "sugah" cookies. We would pull our own weight and help keep our home spotless, leaving a "Martha Stewart" perfect look. Mom walked in at the end of a long day oblivious to the mess Janna and I had gleefully made because Bessie's commanding voice always signaled the end of playtime: "All right girls, time to clean up." And we knew she wasn't asking.

In addition to "raising" us girls, Bessie would periodically alter the routine with one of her "events," which usually involved the use of folk remedies. Bessie was homeopathic before homeopathic was cool. One event in particular stands out. Convinced nature was taking too much of its sweet time, she decided to remove one of my baby teeth that had lingered a bit too long. It became a battle of wills. Who would be stronger, Bessie or that stubborn tooth? With a string knotted onto the object of my discomfort and the far end fastened to the bathroom door knob, "slams" filled the air as my baby tooth stood its ground until I took matters into my own hands, or rather fingers, and wiggled and pulled and wiggled again until that tooth surrendered, with no strings attached.

Now and then, she would take us on walks in the woods to pick "rabbit" tobacco. I remember asking Bessie, "What do you with this stuff?" After a long pause and with a faint smile, she said, "They make a good smoke, especially when I sit on the porch at night and listen to the frogs and crickets."

Bessie filled our home with joy, with the incandescent buoyancy of her spirit and especially with the tangible aroma of peas, potlikker, pork chops, corn bread and pound cake. We always asked her to put the potlikker in a soup bowl to the side. For the uninitiated, potlikker is the juice from peas, collards or turnips – much like boiled peanuts, a culinary delight appreciated mostly by Southern palates. There is no better fed creature on Earth than a Southern child blessed to eat the offerings of someone who knows how to prepare the delights of fresh produce.

While Bessie cooked lunch, she faithfully listened to the gospel radio station, with God's hymns filling her heart. "How Great Thou Art" was her favorite. Oh, how Bessie's witnessing her love for her Lord and Savior filled my heart. Little did I know, Bessie's music would return years later as a part of my solace as I lay in my bedroom fighting fear at the age of 27.

In the 1960s, we referred to Bessie as our colored "maid," a term that saddens me now because it denigrates the dignity of this special lady who raised me and loved me like one of her own.

Our day began with Janna and me riding with Mom to

pick up Bessie. Arriving at Bessie's white clapboard home, Mom would blow the horn signaling we had arrived. Mother always made sure Bessie, Janna and I were safe and sound before she left for work.

Then one April morning in 1973, everything changed. When we arrived at Bessie's home, I sensed something was wrong. Bessie always left her curtains open, but this time, they were drawn tight. Janna and I looked at the front door waiting for our Bessie to move down the steps in her quiet manner, walk to the car and smile a radiant good morning. But time stood hauntingly still as a chilling realization dawned on two suddenly sad little girls.

Bessie was gone.

I remember Janna running with me to the front porch, as Mom called out to Bessie. Finally, Mama pushed opened the door while I held onto the fading hope we would see that gracious smile. Instead, we faced an emptiness matched only by the hole in our spirits. It was as if there had never been a Bessie. Stunned, I reacted like any child who loses a mother: I wept uncontrollably. In my innocence, all I could think was Bessie had left because Janna and I had been "bad" girls. My sister and I fussed and fought a good bit, and I believed Bessie could not stand to be with us a day longer. What else was I to think?

As a little white girl who lived in a white house in a white neighborhood, educated in a white private school, I had no understanding of the challenges Bessie faced as a black woman in the 1960s. The specifics aren't important now, but the vicissitudes of that life had forced a sudden change in Bessie's circumstances. Though she left an aching void in our home, thankfully, Bessie was a strong survivor and remained dedicated to raising her two boys. In the evenings, I would think of how Bessie would love her sons. Her commandments would mold them into Godly men. She would comfort them as her voice lilted from the kitchen and wafted throughout their home, bathing it in peace. When necessary of course, she would flash her "look" to let them know they had crossed the line. I was warmed by these thoughts, knowing my Bessie would be the same insightful inn keeper for her sons as she was for Janna and me.

Bessie Grimes gave us ten wonderful years, and I have many moving memories of her presence in our home. To this day, when I hear "How Great thou Art," I remember desperately wanting her to walk out the door in her starched white uniform, sit beside me in the back seat and hold my hand. That April morning, I lost more than "the help." I lost one of the true loves of my life. So when my daughter, Allison, labeled me a racist, I was heartbroken. But, once again, God took command and gave me the answer I needed:

Jenny Lynn, you will have to tell Allison about 939, but first share the wonderful love story of Bessie with your baby girl. Tell her about this beautiful person who graced your life when you were a little girl yourself. She will understand that you could never harbor such prejudice in your heart. Then, when you tell the rest of your story, she will understand your reaction to the man in the parking lot.

As Allison listened, her countenance radiated peace and understanding, and once again, I felt the powerful reassurance that God knew what He was doing. By the time I finished my story, the harmless man had long since disappeared. Instead, visions of a radiant black woman reaching out to hug her Jenny Lynn silenced the wicked winds of 939.

Scan to hear
**HOW GREAT
THOU ART**

Use a QR Code Reader on
your mobile device

21

Angels

At high noon on September 24, 2010, I took perhaps the second most pivotal step in my post 939 life. The other was when I crossed the threshold of the church sanctuary that first weekend after I limped home from Atlanta. Outwardly, it might appear as if I were turning to the secular, scientific realm, having given up on God's power to exorcise the demons that had tormented me for nearly two decades, but, in reality, He had been leading me to this point for some time. He had been mending me in countless ways, many of which I did not even recognize at the time, for years, and on that radiant Indian summer day, He was at my side as surely as He had been during all the troubled years leading to this moment. The autumn sun suffused the trees lining North College Street with a brilliant, evanescent glow as I readied myself to walk into the office of Dr. Ellen Emerson, licensed psychologist.

Looking through the window of my car, I took cautious note of the parking lot behind Dr. Emerson's office before making my way inside. Hyper-vigilance had long been a perfunctory task for me. I still considered every arena I entered a potential battlefield, so I habitually scouted the terrain to avoid surprise attack. I had come to see, however, that many of the fiends that lay in wait to pounce on me hid in the most unfamiliar territory of all – the deepest recesses of my damaged psyche. This insight had much to do with my decision to see Dr. Emerson.

Before exiting my car, I made one last run through my checklist:

Scope out every inch of the area for possible hiding places.

Stow away anything that might tempt a thief.

Check to make certain car doors are locked.

Scan the area one more time.

Hold pocketbook close and tight.

Walk fast and confidently.

Arrive safely.

Having survived this dash through yet another minefield, I took a deep breath and wondered if I would ever be able to amble about casually and soak in the ambience of new places. What was it somebody said about smelling roses? I wouldn't have noticed they were there. As I crossed the parking lot and entered the office, a faint beam of noonday light gleamed through the doorway, as if God were saying, *"Yes, this is the way."* I believed He had led me to this place and He was going to use Dr. Emerson in a powerful way. In the end, I was right. He had given me the sword of His Spirit, and at times I had wielded it skillfully, but He had also shown me that, though Scripture is complete and perfect, He shines His light in the seemingly secular world, too. So, infused with renewed hope, I walked into Dr. Emerson's office to begin the next chapter in my story.

Mark had always joked that one of the main reasons he married me was I could get ready faster than any woman he had ever known. It's true. I can put on makeup, blow dry my hair, style it, answer a few emails, get a wash of clothes going, and sew on a button for one of the children in 30 minutes flat. Wives and mothers are the quintessential multitaskers. I can see what needs to be done, prioritize the list, and make a move. When I look out at the world and focus on what needs to be done, I am decisive and direct. Administration is definitely one of my spiritual gifts, and I've been a faithful steward, especially in my service to the church: teaching Sunday School, participating in Community Bible Study, and directing Vacation Bible School productions. Over the years, I extended my reach into the community, serving on the boards of United Way, the Statesboro Chamber of Commerce, Leadership Bulloch, and Georgia Southern University's Communication Arts Department.

In a sense, of course, this frenetic pace stems naturally from my personality, but it began to dawn on me that all my dashing to and fro served another purpose as well. I had become quite adept at negotiating my way through the minefields of the external world, but I ignored another, perhaps more dangerous, certainly a more sinister landscape and had allowed the enemy free access to my unconscious mind. I had expended tremendous energy protecting myself from external threats. What I didn't realize for a long time was the herculean psychic effort it took to deny the existence of the enemy who beset me from within.

So, I remained full speed ahead. No one could stop my flight of fright except when Mother occasionally warned me of burn out. She would look at me pleadingly and say, "Jenny Lynn, this fast pace you have always lived is getting totally out of hand. I know you love Mark and the girls, but you've got to get rid of some activities that are running you ragged." Little did she – and for that matter, little did I – know that my dizzying pace was as much to escape as to achieve.

Periodically, I would heed Mom's advice, but not for long. Soon I would fill my calendar to the brim with commitments. Operating in perpetual "overdrive" kept the wolves at bay, but like our psychic reserves, our physical ones are finite. Even during the busiest of days, I would just plain wear out mentally and spiritually, and the rumbling in the attic would become a roar.

For years, Janna had encouraged me to get "help," but I would just hug her and assure her things were okay, or in moments of semi-candor, they would get better. Then on a September evening in 2010, when Mark's saving embrace almost didn't pull me back from the abyss, I finally acknowledged that somewhere deep inside my mind lurked a power I had to face down and defeat. Only, I didn't know how to find it.

I finally opened up just a little in the pre-op suite of Memorial Medical Hospital in Savannah where Janna and I sat waiting while Mother underwent gall bladder surgery. As we discussed Mother's age and condition, the conversation shifted to our own health challenges as we approached our 50th birthdays. We agreed that increasing lack of sleep had begun to take its toll on the two of us. We commiserated about all the factors that kept us from a good night's rest. Warm bedrooms, nocturnal barking dogs, and that last cup of coffee kept us tossing and turning until the wee hours. We pondered these effects and resignedly agreed perfect sleep cycles were a thing of the past. During this light but insightful moment, I finally let my guard down and admitted to Janna what had taken place that September night.

I had gone to bed ahead of Mark with nothing particularly troubling on my mind – at least on the surface. But when Mark entered our bedroom around midnight, to his horror, he saw me in the throes of a death struggle. Creatures from the shadows of my mind had taken advantage of the slumbering, exhausted sentry that was my conscious mind and launched a blood-curdling attack. It took all of Mark's physical and emotional power to wake me from the hellish world I had been plunged into. Consciousness, however, brought me no relief because, as I recounted to Janna, when Mark relived what occurred, I had no memory whatsoever of the nightmarish encounter.

Janna paused, took my hand and said, "Jenny Lynn, you have *got* to get help. You cannot live this way forever." She had made that same entreaty repeatedly for two decades, to no avail, but this time I listened. I knew that as long as I allowed a sanctuary for these monsters where they could hide and plan their terror, I would have no peace. I saw something else that night, too, an image that I did remember: the look on my husband's face, one I had not seen before. It was a mixture of terror and futility. He had always been my rock, strong and implacable – and always hopeful, sure of my ultimate victory. That night, for the first time, I saw doubt and despair. I think maybe for the first time, he began to wonder if he and I would ever return to normalcy. Janna remained calm as I told her about how terror had infiltrated my subconscious and established such a stronghold. Tearfully, I revealed how mine and Mark's bedroom – what should have been our sacred haven – had instead remained a minefield where my next uncontrolled step could set off the explosion that destroyed us for good.

With my load lightened a bit by my admission and with Janna's wise advice echoing in my mind, this time I made a move. The 17th century French philosopher, Blaise Pascal once wrote "All of humanity's problems stem from man's inability to sit quietly in a room alone." I'm sure that statement is layered with meaning, but for me it meant it was time for Jenny Lynn to engage in some guided introspection and face down the intruders that had roamed freely in the recesses of her mind for way too long.

As a start, I reached out to my friend Jack Rainer, our funeral home's grief counselor. I finally had the courage to tell my story openly to someone outside the family. With warmth and concern, he listened until I was completely exhausted. He smiled and asked, "Jenny Lynn, what can I do to help?" As always when we go where God leads, He was in the room with us, and I felt neither embarrassed nor uncomfortable. "Jack," I asked, "is there someone who can help me? Someone who will listen? I need to find my way home." Immediately, he replied, "Jenny Lynn, write down this name: Dr. Ellen Emerson." A disciple of compassion for those who grieve, Jack assured me he would pray and that God would indeed help me find my way back.

And so, I found myself entering a strange, hopeful new world that September day. My optimism matched the radiance of the autumn afternoon as I entered Dr. Emerson's office to begin that stage of my journey where she would be the latest guide the Lord sent me.

The truth will indeed set you free, Jenny Lynn.

You will see.

22

Peeling the Onion

"Grief is a journey, often perilous and without clear direction, that must be taken. The experience of grieving cannot be ordered or categorized, hurried or controlled, pushed aside or ignored indefinitely. It is inevitable as breathing, as change, as love. It may be postponed, but it will not be denied." – Molly Fumia

During that first session with Dr. Emerson, I felt none of the anxiety that usually accompanied any attempt to open up to others, primarily due to her ability to project an air of professional competence coupled with a warm and approachable demeanor. As she asked me to try to talk about that night of terror, I sensed a surge of confidence – a distantly familiar, albeit lately, a rather phantom sensation – and began the story of my years in the wilderness. That cathartic narration began to chip away at the wall 20 years of paralyzing fear had erected around me.

When the appointment was over, I caught myself still looking for the black man as I walked to my car, but the strangest thing distracted me. I noticed what a glorious afternoon it was. For just a moment, I could say with the Christian poet Gerard Manley Hopkins "The world is charged with the grandeur of God." His beautiful blue sky and His glorious sun bathed the road home to Mark and the girls.

To prepare for our next session, Dr. Emerson asked if I would write in long hand how this event had impacted my life. Seeing the doubt in my expression, she smiled and assured me that I would do a good job. A few years ago, Christian apologist and evangelist Ravi Zacharias penned a devotion on the therapeutic power of this kind of writing:

> For the past decade, doctors and psychologists have been taking notice of the health benefits of reflective writing. They note that wrestling with words to put your deepest thoughts into writing can lift your mind from depression, uncover wisdom within your experiences, provide insight and foster self-awareness. Similarly, a recent news article discussed the benefits of confessional writing, where one is freed to "explore the depths of the emotional junkyard." While writing is no doubt a helpful way to sift through the junkyard, its effectiveness is perhaps dependent upon learning from reflection, not merely reveling in the messes... Writing is helpful because the eye of a writer seeks the transcendent--moments where the extraordinary is beheld in the ordinary, glimpses of clarity within the junkyard, the beauty of God in a godless world... There is something about writing that can introduce us to ourselves and to the one in whose image we are made. Have you dared to utter the words at the center of your soul? What if God could use your own pen to probe the wounds of your life? (A Slice of Infinity December 31, 2002)

That evening I began the journey into the past with a new sense of place. As I wrestled with those 20 years, my writing did indeed begin to loosen the chains that had bound me and to clear away the debris in my "emotional junkyard."

During the second session, Dr. Emerson sat across from me unmoved as I read the impact statement to her. When I finished, she asked, "Jenny Lynn, how do you feel right now?" I told her I felt nothing – neither fear's grip nor joy's embrace. She responded, "Jenny Lynn, let's examine your 'stuck points,' the false beliefs that have developed as a result of the trauma. Many trauma victims feel it is their fault. They believe they could have done something different to prevent the assault." That idea, fortunately, had never entered my mind. I knew I had done all that was humanly possible to fight the man. No, guilt wasn't the "stuck point" I had fixated on since 939.

For the first time in two decades, I felt the courage to open up because I knew my listener, although compassionate, would remain objective. I leaned forward, faced Dr. Emerson, and gave voice to one of my biggest fears, a lie whose tendrils had grown deep into my mind:

"I believe my spirit and joy were destroyed that night. I believe I will never be safe again. I believe I 'lost' Jenny Lynn."

Placing her notes by her side, she said, "Jenny Lynn, you have to establish new beliefs, ones that mirror reality. There are ways to stop the pattern of problematic thinking." I had never considered I could rewire my brain to rid myself of these self-defeating habitual thoughts, but using a powerful technique called cognitive therapy, one can do just that.

She then asked me to go home and record every detail of what happened the night of November 28, 1990. Later as she listened to my narrative, Dr. Emerson offered a stunning insight: All these years, I had focused on the sexual assault, when in truth it was the robbery that had caused the majority of my anxiety and post traumatic stress. She supported her shocking assertion by reminding me of my dashing to the car and hurriedly locking the doors, constantly checking my purse, and remaining ever watchful for that face in the crowd.

I left Atlanta panic-stricken at the thought the man would find me and finish what he had started in Room 939, but not until I began reflecting on Dr. Emerson's pronouncement did I connect my fear with robbery instead of sexual assault. Then, I remembered the wedding ring I had frantically hidden from him. I had lain on that floor heartbroken at the thought of the most tangible symbol of my marriage to Mark leaving the room in the hands of a monster. That was his unfinished business! I had walled myself in emotionally. He couldn't touch me there, but my material possessions were visible and vulnerable – objects there for the taking – especially the token of our eternal love for one another.

"What God has joined together, let no man put asunder" (Mark 10:9).

By no means did her revelation diminish the damage done to my soul by the sexual assault. Rather, she enabled me to step back and see the total picture. Later that afternoon, as I stood looking at a portrait of my family taken at the beach, I wasn't yet sure I could completely buy into what Dr. Emerson had told me, but I knew I had found someone who would walk the long road home with me. If I accepted her offer to come along on my journey, I just might recover the lady in the picture with the radiant smile and the beautiful, blessed family.

As our sessions continued, Dr. Emerson asked me to keep writing about 939. "Everything," she said. "I want it all. Don't leave anything out!" I maintained control throughout my readings, but I must admit I fought back tears when I came to my final paragraph: *"To this day I want the old Jenny Lynn back. Wouldn't it be great to live that life again? But I know the truth. She is gone and will never knock on my door again. I miss her every day."* I still believed Satan, the liar.

Dr. Emerson met my admission with another profound observation. "Jenny Lynn," she said, "your loss of self and loss of joy have led to grieving. Your experience has been more grief than fear." With a look of disbelief, I quipped, "Dr. Emerson, my husband has owned a funeral home for 15 years. Grief is nothing new to me."

But, she pointed out, I had been focusing on the grief of others, which while commendable, had also kept me from recognizing my own. "While you could associate with everyone else's grief, you were unable to identify your own because it was buried in a state of denial." Then, she explained the five steps of grief: **Denial/Isolation, Sadness/Depression, Bargaining, Anger, and Acceptance.** Here's what they mean to me:

> **1. Denial and Isolation.** *I wanted to deny the loss took place. I wanted to escape my torment. I withdrew from all who loved me. Much like those in the community who didn't know how to approach me soon after the assault, a part of me believed that if I could ignore it, it hadn't really happened. And, letting others into my life made that denial much harder to pull off.*

> **2. Sadness and Depression.** *The innate energy that had enabled me to approach life with excitement and anticipation was gone, used up in my efforts at denial.*

> **3. Bargaining.** *I told God I would change anything and everything in my life if He would remove my pain, replacing it with peace. Now I know we can't bargain with God. What in the world could we offer Him*

anyway, other than to say yes to his grace? Yes, Lord.
Yes, yes.

4. Anger. *I hated what the invader did to me. I hated the emotional scars. Anger also drains energy. See number 2.*

5. Acceptance. *I had yet to accept the reality of my loss. Instead, I had believed I had lost something no man can take away from me, my true identity in Christ. Dr. Emerson confirmed Acceptance was the one step I had not experienced.*

With grief confirmed as the cause of my emotional paralysis, I was able to complete the list by accepting the reality of my loss ... no more denial. I could now identify grief's devastating toll. Grief was a constant drain on my energy, entrapping me in depression. It took away the normalcy of life leaving my existence a mere shadow. It became clear to me why every day ended in defeat. I was battling fear, not grief. Focusing on the wrong enemy, I left both flanks wide open, vulnerable to the enemy's incessant attacks.

I had been terribly damaged that night, and I had surely suffered irreparable loss. I had lost the innocent joy that an imperfect, yet lovely childhood had given me. I had been stripped of the unbridled optimism that led me to believe I would always navigate smooth seas, hindered only occasionally here and there by a minor tempest. Life would not always follow the script I had written. But by not grieving, I had allowed my suffering to transmogrify into a gargantuan pack of lies that had swallowed me whole. Consequently, I could not see the truth of what God still had in store for me:

Lie: The old Jenny Lynn is lost and gone forever.

Truth: Though battered, bruised, the essence of

Jenny Lynn cannot be touched. She came home from Atlanta different, definitely damaged, but her broken places will knit together stronger than before. The real Jenny Lynn is *"hid with Christ in God"* (Colossians 3:3).

Lie: The world is a dangerous place where evil roars about free to ravish whom it wishes.

Truth: The world is fallen and can be a dangerous place but no more so than the day before I left for that conference. And, most importantly, *"Underneath are the everlasting arms"* (Deuteronomy 33:27).

Lie: Life's joys and blessings were not for me. I would smile through the pain and genuinely enjoy the successes of friends and family, but I would have to live out my life encased in a callous shell to protect myself from disappointment.

Truth: The road home to Statesboro for Mother and me that weekend 20 years ago led back to a lovely home, to two yet to be born beautiful daughters who would bring their parents inexpressible joy, an extended family that loves me unconditionally, a treasure chest of good friends, and eventually church homes where I would grow in the knowledge of my Lord and Savior, Jesus Christ.

Lie: I would never be of use to God.

Truth: *I have a ministry for you Jenny Lynn. You will write about your life and you will speak to others of My grace. As my servant Paul wrote to Timothy, "Do not neglect your gift, which was given you"* (I Timothy 4:14). *Time to get at it, don't you think?*

Concerning grief, Jack Rainer offers this advice: "No one has the right to take grief from us. It is deserved and if we embrace it, there is the assurance it will lead to peace. Grief is like having a broken leg. No one is going to criticize using crutches until healing is complete. Grief blessed by time will bring that day of healing."

Now as I experience renewal and freedom, I agree totally with Jack. We cannot avoid grief, but only through our individual steps in His grace do we become involved in the healing process. Sadly, too many of us seek a quick fix, and as a result, the grief never goes away. Neither does sadness nor our sense of loss.

Enlightened and reenergized after 14 weeks with Dr. Emerson and Jack's encouragement, I grew confident I could walk down this path of healing and do what God has called me to. I close this chapter with yet more exhortation from the Apostle Paul: *"Let us not become weary in doing good, for at the proper time we will reap a harvest if we do not give up"* (Galatians 6:9). With God's grace, I will not give up.

23

Confirmation

"I can do all things through Christ who strengthens me."
Philippians 4:13

As we ended our discussion on grief, Dr. Emerson saved her most convincing fact for last: "Jenny Lynn, do you have any idea how you endured your trials all those years without seeking support from those who loved you the most?" I remembered the direct look on her face as she added without hesitation, "You were not a victim. You were a survivor."

Me, Jenny Lynn, a survivor? I recalled my friend's having offered me that description earlier, but now Dr. Emerson's pronouncement confirmed this truth.

Later that afternoon, as I sat in the comfort of my den, His Scriptures came to me. I recalled God's intervening on the Israelites' behalf when all seemed lost, the Red Sea ahead and the Egyptian army behind. God's strength enabled me to triumph as a survivor and freed me from a lifetime of bondage.

I do admit I remained ignorant of His saving grace for too long, yet I must also remember the Israelites wandered in the wilderness for 40 years. Though they doubted, and feared, and complained, they nevertheless remained His chosen people. And now, all who call upon His name are in that select company. God knows our heart. He knows us better than we do ourselves. One day long ago, a child gave her heart to Jesus as she listened to Mrs. Beasley tell her Sunday School class about her great Friend. From that moment, the little girl's life was sealed. Yes, she would stray and doubt – and keep God at arm's length sometimes – but the Lord never let her out of His sight, no, not really. Now, I'm comfortable telling others about my Savior. To the broken-hearted, the book of Hebrews encourages us who must persevere to keep our eyes fixed on Jesus, the only one who can perfect and finish our faith journey. Knowing the joy that would come in joining His Father, The Almighty God, Jesus could disregard the shame endured before His death on the cross. We have to reflect on this event each time we *"grow weary and lose heart"* (Hebrews 12: 2-3).

Indeed, let us not lose heart.

24

Finding My Voice

"There is a time for everything,
and a season for every activity under the heavens:
a time to be born and a time to die,
a time to plant and a time to uproot,
a time to kill and a time to heal,
a time to tear down and a time to build,
a time to weep and a time to laugh,
a time to mourn and a time to dance,
a time to scatter stones and a time to gather them,
a time to embrace and a time to refrain from embracing,
a time to search and a time to give up,
a time to keep and a time to throw away,
a time to tear and a time to mend,
a time to be silent and a time to speak,
a time to love and a time to hate,
a time for war and a time for peace."
Ecclesiastes 3

Though the knife pressing against my throat did no physical damage, the trauma of those 15 minutes left me absent of a voice once powerful and generous. For the next 20 years, my fight to recover my sense of self sapped me of vitality and vivacity. Lost in a sea of pain and doubt, I had no voice to help others with their struggles. How could I exhort others to face seemingly insurmountable odds when hope burned so dimly in my own soul? I wanted desperately to inspire my friends to believe in their dreams. I wanted to help my community prosper.

Most of all, I wanted to tell others about the God I had found midst my heartache and suffering. With the Lord's faithfulness, Mark and I managed to raise two strong, confident daughters, but I had little energy left to be a strong voice for my friends, church, and community. In many ways, those 15 minutes left me mute.

For the past 20 years, I have wrestled with doubt, with fear, with anger, and perhaps, most of all, I have wrestled with my stalwart choice not to forgive. My story is about recovery and redemption, triumph and joy. I want so much for it to be a beacon of hope for those who see no way out of their pain. Most of all, I want them to know the God who continues to heal me, to understand the truths He has taught me about Himself – and about myself. Maybe you believe yours is the one situation He cannot or will not fix, that your enemy is too powerful. Or perhaps, you believe you are beyond God's generous free gift of grace, for whatever reason you are not worthy. Those are the devil's lies!

Please understand He is patient. He knows us – our struggles, our strengths, and our weaknesses – better than we know ourselves. If He is who He says He is, then you cannot disappoint Him. In His omniscience, He knows all you have done, all you have left undone, and all you will do. On the night He was betrayed, Jesus told Peter, "before the rooster crows, you will disown me three times" (Matthew 26:34). The Lord was not disappointed when Peter failed him because He already knew what was in Peter's heart. He also knew it would be Peter who would be the rock – the foundation of His church. He had given that commission to Peter before that dark night and reaffirmed it in front of the other disciples shortly before His ascension. Christ knew what Peter could and would do, not because of this brash fisherman's own strength, but because of the rivers of living water He would pour through Peter to bless others. He is pouring those waters through me now. He will do the same in your life. He will never give up on those who come to Him for salvation and the often long and arduous process of sanctification, our growth in grace. He *will* complete the work He began in you. Do not doubt that.

We, on the other hand, are not so patient. Even the strongest, most faithful Christians endure seasons – not just moments – of darkness. We lose heart when God does not appear to be working in the way we expect or according to our timing. We drift away during the tough times, and perhaps more dangerously, many of us forget about Him when things are great. Then, there are the times He tests us – not to learn anything about us – He knows exactly what and who we are – but to teach us truths we can learn in no other way. He does not deliver us from trouble. He delivers us *in* trouble. Some of our wounds are self-inflicted; some come at the hands of others. Some arise from unfathomable mysteries. He will heal them all.

Yes, He can heal the heart broken in a thousand pieces with merely a touch, or He can put the fragments back together bit by bit over many years. The timing is up to Him, but I do know one thing: the mending process speeds up in direct proportion to our trust and obedience. For me, trusting was the most difficult. Because I did not know the Lord very well before 939, my faith grew in fits and starts, the proverbial two steps forward, one step backward. I had so much to learn about God and His ways.

For years, I missed one very important point. God in his inexhaustible patience, however, kept gently leading me to the place where I would see. Because I did not really know how to grieve over what I had lost – or what had been stolen from me – I failed to understand without death there can be no resurrection. I searched in vain for the old Jenny Lynn, and it nearly crushed my spirit to think I'd never find her. But here's the rub. In a sense, God didn't want me to find her! He wanted to resurrect the new creature, the Jenny Lynn born again in Christ! He wanted to show the world the new and improved Jenny Lynn, while I kept looking for the old model! Or maybe it is more apt to say He wanted me to recover my "old self" so I could lay that life down and find my eternal life, my true self in Christ.

And so, I kept fighting for my voice, and on a spring afternoon in 2010, God delivered me a mighty victory. Oh, did He ever! Sitting on my patio with a copy of *The George Anne*, Georgia Southern's student newspaper, I began reading about "Operation Clothesline," a campus forum on rape and sexual assault. Victims would be encouraged to inscribe their messages of molestation on t-shirts. I was more than ready to share. I had the commitment, I had the courage, and as I read that article, I felt my voice roaring to life.

Laura Milner, a professor in Georgia Southern's Department of Writing and Linguistics, coordinated "Operation Clothesline." Laura and I had become friends when she served as Statesboro's Bureau Chief for the *Savannah News-Press* in the early 1990s. We were kindred spirits in many ways, one being our mutual dedication to alleviating the suffering caused by drug and alcohol abuse. Over the years Laura impressed me with her courage and unwavering commitment to the issues she championed. Her passion and indomitable spirit inspired me. With her at the helm, I knew "Operation Clothesline" would reach many hurting – and mute – souls.

As always, God had perfect timing. In less than a

year, Morgan, now a high school senior, would be going away to college, so I wanted her to attend "Operation Clothesline" with me. I remember the strength in my voice when I told her, "Morgan, your eyes will be opened when you see the healing taking place in the faces of these wounded women. I want you to be aware sexual violence will always be a threat to women." We both understood my point.

The day we assembled in the Georgia Southern Rotunda, it was alive with a steady stream of visitors and university students. Tension filled the air as Morgan and I made our way through the heavy parade of multi-colored t-shirts scripted to give voices to those silenced by rape and assault.

The number of t-shirts hanging in the round, concrete space stopped me in my tracks.

Oh, Lord, so many bruised and battered souls! So many lives nearly destroyed by some deranged man! Lord have mercy on us all. Lord, please heal us all.

The magnitude of this cruelty had never really dawned on me until that spring afternoon when I came face to face with these powerful visuals. I walked the rotunda, reading every memo of rape and assault. Each declaration roared injustice, despair and brokenness. One shirt screamed "Just because I danced with you doesn't mean I wanted to F*CK you! Another cried, "You may have bent me, but you did not BREAK me! Because of the Hell you put me through I am stronger." There it was. Banner after banner laid bare the gamut of emotions I had felt for years: pain, anger, resentment, defiance.

I could barely breathe.

Seeing this demonstration of devastation, my visceral reaction to this heartrending spectacle was that it was time for Jenny Lynn to deal with her pent-up fury. So, with shirt and pen in hand, I was ready to unleash my hostility. Then a lump formed in my throat. As I paused and stared at the empty canvas, I felt God stir in my heart. Most of the women at the forum were much younger than I and their wounds much fresher. I understood and totally sympathized with their powerful sentiments, especially the anger and resentment. I knew a forum like this would be an important step in their journeys home. But I saw something else as well. Though I did not judge these young women for the angry messages screaming from their banners, I knew these ravaged souls would have no peace until they took the next, infinitely more difficult step: releasing their bitterness and replacing it with forgiveness.

With forgiveness, I could now move forward. With forgiveness, I could release my desire for revenge as I now accepted His Scripture's promise: *"The Lord will judge his people."*

I uncapped the pen and in large letters, blessed the shirt: *November 28, 1990. You are Forgiven.*

With Morgan beside me, I added my t-shirt to the army of cloth warriors filling the rotunda. I turned and looked into my daughter's eyes. She knew her mother was back. No longer would bitterness, shame and regret create shadows in our home. From this day forward, I would shower my girls with a love undiluted by the unhealed wounds of 939. Life was now a green light. Forgiveness had swept away the last remnants of my hatred. In that moment I felt God's deliverance and my resurrection. I was indeed a new creation!

**Scan to see images from
OPERATION CLOTHESLINE**

Use a QR Code Reader on
your mobile device

25

Walking in His Light

Saturday morning, November 27, 2010

Jazz music provides the lively ambience in the Au Pied de Cochon, the Intercontinental Hotel's Restaurant in Buckhead, an upscale neighborhood of Atlanta. The luxury hotel's windows offer a view of the city's tree-lined pulse, Peachtree Street – a majestic corridor of steel, glass, and manicured sidewalks. As the dawning sun shines on the skyscrapers, a kaleidoscope of autumn colors entertains me as I sit at 6:30 a.m., the lone customer sipping coffee in a cavernous dining room. Wistfully, I remember this was once my favorite time of year. I met my husband in the fall. I got married in the fall. I came alive in the fall.

My burden lightened by so many of God's graces – forgiveness, Dr. Emerson's wise insights, my friend Jack's loving counsel, the company of my wonderful husband and beautiful daughters – I suddenly realize I have the courage to make the journey back to the *chamber*. It's just a few miles away from where I now sit, but for a long time it was a boulevard of no return. As Mark, our girls and I planned our Atlanta weekend shopping trip, I had no idea I would feel this powerful surge of courage and urge to drive the stake once and for all into the heart of 939.

I vividly remember how, in 1990, my declaration was I would *never* find the strength to return to the hotel's ninth floor. Yet, every time we passed through downtown

Atlanta during those 20 years, I would look at the hotel looming in the distant skyline, count to the ninth floor, and fixate on that corner room.

Saturday evening, November 27, 2010

Mark, Morgan, Allison and I travel down International Boulevard toward the hotel. Mark parks the car near the valet area and tells the bell hop we are here to pick up a guest. We agree our teenage daughters will stay in the car while Mark and I take our final steps.

A large wedding group fills the lobby. Women and young girls radiate joy in their designer saris. A mother fusses over a daughter's dress. A rainbow of jeweled colors dances about the room shouting hope and anticipation. As Mark and I move through the laughter and celebration, I am thankful for the buzz that allows me to slip unnoticed through the crowds. It is as if we are on a secret mission to retrieve something from that 9th floor. Maybe we are.

This same lobby was to have been the rendezvous point for an important meeting with an editor. It never happened. Mark and I enter the elevator and within seconds arrive at the 9th floor. The doors slide open. A pungent blend of curry mixed with the heavy staleness of old property permeates the hallway. As we make our way down the quiet hall, Mark comments on its length. I note the lighting seems better. Eerily, it is as if each room number beckons me. I am counting ... 931 ... 933 ... 935 ... 937 ... I pass by the stairwell where the dark man made his escape.

Now I am standing in front of 939. Nothing has changed. I cannot help wondering how many guests have enjoyed 939 in the past 20 years. But what does that matter? It is time for resolution. I remain poised as I stand and remember – the knife, the enforcement, the captivity. Mark senses what is taking place and remains silent, aware he has no words to add to the moment.

Turning and again taking in the vastness of the corridor, I am filled with a rush of anger and despair, those demons that have tormented me for 20 years sensing one last chance at the victory that was never to be theirs. When I screamed, why didn't those guests who stepped from their rooms come to my rescue? Surely they heard my pleading—the sounds of human terror. Why did they allow peril rather than peace to carry that day? How much torment have I endured because they did not want to get involved?

But now I see the answer to that lingering question.

At the end of the hallway, just before 939 and 940, a door casing protrudes from each side of the corridor creating an alcove for these last two rooms. It suddenly dawns on me my neighbors weren't indifferent or afraid that night. They simply couldn't see the man holding me captive.

Mark and I look from 939 to the elevator's waiting area. Mark then opens the door to the emergency stairwell. He stares. I have no idea what my husband is thinking. Interrupting his thoughts, I ask him to estimate the length of the corridor.

"Jenny Lynn, this is at least one football field or more. Why?"

"Because I want to know the exact distance my screams were heard." We decide to measure. As I begin counting my strides to the elevator, I know I am finally leaving the long-lived destruction behind me. My legs are strong. I can breathe, not gasp. Vision clear, I see life now in full detail.

My steps are light in my gray, suede boots. At 47, I feel hip and stylish. Happiness does that. Mark accompanies me in silence as I count out loud, my voice resonating throughout the hallway. Completing my measured walk, I approximate 270 feet. Did the sound of my screams travel nearly the length of a football field? Yes.

The bustling lobby greets us again. Life in the big city continues its beat, just as it had that night. As we leave the hotel, I take a moment to think about how much I love my husband and the life we have created together. I slide into the front seat and look at my beautiful daughters. I have come full circle. Once again, I savor a renewed excitement for metropolitan life and the promise big cities offer small-town girls from rural Georgia. A Michael Buble song fills our car as we head north on Peachtree Street. Morgan and Allison sing in the back seat. Mark opens the sun roof and the world embraces us. I feel the cold, dry air whipping through my hair on this crisp fall night. I look up at the skyscraper lights, which create the wonderful aura of the Noel season. How appropriate. Peachtree Street seems to stretch to the uttermost boundary of the horizon, a symbol of beckoning hope. Then, amid all the noise and excitement, I hear a familiar voice:

Do you see that, Jenny Lynn? It's the future. I have many plans for you? Are you ready?

Yes, Lord! I'm ready!

Scan to hear
A PEACE WITHIN

Use a QR Code Reader on
your mobile device

6/26/2011

Dear Invader,

In my 48 years of life, I have never addressed a letter to a person without a name, but in this case, I have no other choice. I have never known your name. I have never known your age. I have never known your address. I have never known anything about you – only that on November 28, 1990, you would enter a downtown Atlanta hotel and completely alter a woman's life – my life.

For many years, your facial composite created by the forensic sketch artist lay buried in a file. I could not look at your face. Too much hurt, too much pain. It only reminded me of what I did not want to accept ... that when you captured me, you locked me into a prison that had no key. No escape.

I want you to know what prison feels like. You never feel safe. Your world is a cubicle of pain. Its walls of suffering are endless. It reeks of devastation. Its darkness has no security. The screams of agony are ceaseless. Its solitude makes you mute ... changes you into someone unrecognizable to the people who love you most.

This place becomes your deathbed.

Because my pain was so excruciating and you encased my soul with shame, I chose solitary confinement, allowing only morsels of sustenance from my family and friends. They tried so hard to reach me, but I refused their love and support. They could not comfort me in this place they knew nothing about.

Scan to hear
JENNY LYNN
READING LETTER

Use a QR Code Reader on
your mobile device

But you get to the point in prison where the walls begin to suffocate you and you realize peace will never come unless you rely on something greater than yourself. You look through that tiny crack where light streams in and you cry out for God to come and deliver you.

And that's exactly what God did.

He looked down on me and said, "Jenny Lynn. I know you are hurting, but if you will trust in Me, I will show you how to bring peace to your storm. I will heal you if you will let me help you."

I am ashamed to admit this, but I didn't believe God had enough power to remove the shackles you had placed on me and I continued to run from Him.

But the faster I ran, the more God began putting speed bumps along the way. He did it for years and years. He was mightily creative, placing people and messages in my path to slow the race. And finally, I was so exhausted, so weary, I looked up and told God I could no longer push Him away. God said, "If you'll listen to me, I'm going to show you the way out of prison."

And He did.

God told me I would never be able to love myself again until I forgave you. So I retrieved your picture and looked at you for a long time. I did not rush. I memorized all the lines of your face, the shape of your almond eyes, every feature of the being God created. And then something happened. God softened my heart and I saw you for the first time as a man who was wrought with hurt and pain. I felt sorry for you, for how you were deeply wounded in your life. Perhaps someone hurt you badly when you were little and shaped you into a man of hate ... I do not know. The only thing I know for certain is you can ask God for forgiveness, too. God forgives all sinners. When God looks down on humanity, He does not measure sin the way we humans do. We always think some sins are worse than others. That's not true. Sin is sin. By asking God to forgive you for hurting me in 1990, He completely erases that night and you can start anew. Your life is pure again, white as snow. God will never leave you or forsake you.

That I know for sure because I no longer walk on a solitary path. He is with me every day and I am now complete again because of His love. The peace our Creator has given me is offered to you as well. My prayer is that you may someday feel His presence in your life and that your journey will become one of hope and healing as mine has.

I leave you with a Bible verse if you are still running from our Almighty God. I have read this Scripture over and over for many years and hope it will bring you the promises of His faithfulness. If you have not already found God ... He waits for you.

Where can I go from your Spirit? Where can I flee from your presence? If I go up to the heavens, you are there; if I make my bed in the depths, you are there. If I rise on the wings of dawn, if I settle on the far side of the sea, even there your hand will guide me, your right hand will hold me fast. If I say, "Surely the darkness will hide me and the light become night around me," even the darkness will not be dark to you; the night will shine like the day, for darkness is as light to you (Psalm 139:7-12).

May God bless you,

Jenny Lynn

Scriptural Reflections

By Dr. John Waters, Pastor

First Baptist Church, Statesboro, GA

Going Places: *Therefore do not worry about tomorrow, for tomorrow will worry about itself. Each day has enough trouble of its own.* Matthew 6:34

Room 939: *I am overwhelmed with troubles and my life draws near to death. I am counted among those who go down to the pit; I am like one without strength.* Psalm 88:3-4

Blueprint: *I praise you because I am fearfully and wonderfully made; your works are wonderful, I know that full well.* Psalm 139:14a

The Rock: *Blessed is the one who does not walk in step with the wicked or stand in the way that sinners take or sit in the company of mockers, but whose delight is in the law of the LORD, and who meditates on his law day and night. That person is like a tree planted by streams of water, which yields its fruit in season and whose leaf does not wither – whatever they do prospers. Not so the wicked! They are like chaff that the wind blows away. Therefore the wicked will not stand in the judgment, nor sinners in the assembly of the righteous. For the LORD watches over the way of the righteous, but the way of the wicked leads to destruction.* Psalm 1

Valley of Death: *The engulfing waters threatened me, the deep surrounded me; seaweed was wrapped around my head.* Jonah 2:5

Spiritual Awakening: *"This is the covenant I will make with the people of Israel after that time," declares the LORD. "I will*

put my law in their minds and write it on their hearts. I will be their God, and they will be my people." Jeremiah 31:33

Living, Loving, and Learning: *Do you not know that your bodies are temples of the Holy Spirit, who is in you, whom you have received from God? You are not your own.* 1 Corinthians 6:19

War Zone: *LORD, how many are my foes! How many rise up against me!* Psalm 3:1

Turbulence: *You will not fear the terror of night, nor the arrow that flies by day.* Psalm 91:5

My Faithful Father: *Keep your lives free from the love of money and be content with what you have, because God has said, "Never will I leave you; never will I forsake you."* Hebrews 13:5

Happy Faces: *Will you never look away from me, or let me alone even for an instant?* Job 7:19

Tug of War: *For I am convinced that neither death nor life, neither angels nor demons, neither the present nor the future, nor any powers, neither height nor depth, nor anything else in all creation, will be able to separate us from the love of God that is in Christ Jesus our Lord.* Romans 8:38-39

The Girls: *"For I know the plans I have for you," declares the LORD, "plans to prosper you and not to harm you, plans to give you hope and a future."* Jeremiah 29:11

My BFF (Best Friend Forever): *"Before I formed you in the womb I knew you, before you were born I set you apart; I appointed you as a prophet to the nations."* Jeremiah 1:5

Revelation: *"If you forgive anyone's sins, their sins are forgiven; if you do not forgive them, they are not forgiven."* John 20:23

Almighty God: *God is our refuge and strength, an ever-present help in trouble.* Psalm 46:1

For He Waits: *Your word is a lamp for my feet, a light on my path.* Psalm 119:105

Reversal: *The teaching of the wise is a fountain of life, turning a person from the snares of death.* Proverbs 13:14

Down Time: *Though he slay me, yet will I hope in him; I will surely defend my ways to his face.* Job 13:15

The Truth: *A wife of noble character who can find? She is worth far more than rubies.* Proverbs 31:10

Angels: *For his anger lasts only a moment, but his favor lasts a lifetime; weeping may stay for the night, but rejoicing comes in the morning.* Psalm 30:5

Peeling the Onion: *Blessed are those who mourn, for they will be comforted.* Matthew 5:4

Confirmation: *I can do all this through him who gives me strength.* Philippians 4:13

Finding My Voice: *He who was seated on the throne said, "I am making everything new!" Then he said, "Write this down, for these words are trustworthy and true."* Revelation 21:5

Walking in His Light: *Who shall separate us from the love of Christ? Shall trouble or hardship or persecution or famine or nakedness or danger or sword? ... No, in all these things we are more than conquerors through him who loved us.* Romans 8:35, 37

Book Club Questions

1. We will all have to overcome many obstacles in life. What is the greatest obstacle to your faith? How did you face this challenge?

2. In Room 939, Jenny Lynn used her faith by calling on God to escape the invader. What do you typically do when in a difficult circumstance? Recall, too, that Jenny Lynn had not been close to God for years, yet she called on Him in her moment of terror. Many of us instinctively cry to God when we are in intense pain. However, perhaps it is even more difficult to seek Him when life is mundane and the rigors of everyday life, those drab, grey days in the valley, wear us down. Which is harder for you, the crisis or the routine?

3. Jenny Lynn speaks of her struggles to reconcile the God who loves with the God who brings judgment. Have you wrestled with this issue? Which God is more real to you?

4. Self-reliance is a dominant characteristic that kept Jenny Lynn from accepting God's grace and giving her life to Him. It's what theologians call that "satanic right to ourselves" that first appeared in the Garden of Eden. After years of struggle, however, Jenny Lynn came to realize that she was fighting to hold onto her old self when God wanted to make her a "new creation," which ironically would transform her into her truest self. What trait deters you from allowing God to guide you from your darkness? Are you afraid that if you submit to God you will lose your identity? Jesus says that "He who loses his life for My sake will find it." Do you believe that?

5. Forgiving is a challenging assignment for everyone. Jenny Lynn's unwillingness to forgive blocked her growth

and her healing. Are you unable to forgive someone, perhaps even yourself? Can you relate to what Jenny Lynn learned about the true nature of forgiveness? What can you do now to begin the process of forgiving?

6. Her fear caused Jenny Lynn to build a protective shield around herself, one that kept even her loved ones at a "safe" distance. Is fear keeping you from living your life to the fullest? Or is it anxiety, pessimism, or depression? Could it be something else?

7. Jenny Lynn describes her experiences in church, some good, others uncomfortable. Unfortunately, experiences in church keep many doubters from coming to Christ. What have your experiences in church been like? If they have been hurtful, would you be willing to seek others who have had similar trials? In truth, church attendance is not a gateway to heaven, though many seem to believe it is just that. What does the church mean to you? What does worship mean to you? Is it something you do for a couple of hours on Sunday morning? Do you worship in every area of your life?

8. Jenny Lynn struggled to regain her faith. Fear is the enemy of faith and love. What is the greatest obstacle to your faith? Fear? Lack of forgiveness? Feelings of worthlessness?

9. Jenny Lynn, in recalling her trials of being a normal loving mother for Morgan and Allison, found His song "Little Ones to Him Belong" her saving grace as she battled the evils of fear and doubt. How does His word resonate in your life as a parent when threatened by fear and doubt?

Notes

CHAPTER 6

Excerpt from <u>Robert Frost Selected Poems</u> (Copyright 1992, Random House).

CHAPTER 10

Prayer reproduced in <u>People of the Lie</u> by Charles K. Robinson.

CHAPTER 13

Quotes from <u>The Business of Heaven: Daily Readings from C. S. Lewis</u> (ed. Walter Hooper; 1984, Harcourt, Brace, Jovanovich).

CHAPTER 14

Quote from Oswald Chambers taken from <u>My Utmost for His Highest</u> (Copyright 1935, Dodd, Mead & Company).

CHAPTER 15

Quote from <u>The Business of Heaven: Daily Readings from C. S. Lewis</u> (ed. Walter Hooper; 1984, Harcourt, Brace, Jovanovich).

CHAPTER 16

Scripture Quote from <u>The Message: The New Testament in Contemporary English</u> (Copyright 1993 by Eugene Peterson).

CHAPTER 22

Quote from Molly Fumia taken from www.griefsjourney.com.

Quote from December 31, 2002, edition of A Slice of Infinity, a daily email devotion from Ravi Zacharias International Ministries (RZIM) Copyright (c).

Jenny Lynn Anderson

During her 25 years as a corporate journalist, Jenny Lynn Anderson established and maintained a highly respected reputation for her evocative reporting, allowing her readers ease in absorbing her messages.

This first-time author is a 1985 graduate of Georgia Southern University, majoring in Public Relations. Jenny Lynn resides in Statesboro, Georgia, with her husband, Mark, and daughters, Morgan and Allison. Currently, she serves as a private consultant in the areas of marketing and public relations.

Ric Mandes

During his 40-year career as a writer, Ric Mandes served as Director of Institutional Development for Georgia Southern College and later as Senior Vice President, Southeastern Marketing Services. Mandes is retired and lives in Statesboro, Georgia.